Getting
Passion
Out of Your Profession

To Kerry!
So lovely to meet &
chat with you enroute!.
Keep Working with
Passion !
Steven Spencer
Mar 27/07

Getting
Passion
Out of Your Profession

How to keep loving your living...
come what may

Nina Spencer
Author of the acclaimed newsletter "Working Wisdom"

Transcontinental Metrolitho Book Group
Sherbrooke, Quebec, Canada, 2006

GETTING PASSION OUT OF YOUR PROFESSION:
How to keep loving your living...come what may

Copyright © 2006 by Nina Spencer

First Edition, 2006
Third Printing, December, 2006

National Library of Canada Cataloguing in Publication

Spencer, Nina, 1957 –
          Getting Passion Out of Your Profession: How to keep loving your living...come what may

Includes index and bibliographical references.

ISBN 0-9737102-0-9

1. Work success--psychological aspects. 2. Self-actualization--psychology. 3. Motivation.
4. Job satisfaction and career development. 5. Life skills. 6. Business communications/relations.
7. Personal and positional leadership. I. Title

HF5549.5 J63 S633 2005   158.7 21   C2005-9063688

This book is available at special discount for bulk purchases by your group, company, organization or professional association, for sales or event promotions, premiums, fundraising or professional/management development workshop presentations.

For details please call: 416-588-3334
email: nina@ninaspencer.com or visit: www.ninaspencer.com

Cover Design, Text Design and Layout: Bernard Hellen, Traffic Marketing + Design, Toronto

Development/Managing Editor: Brian Broderson

Project Manager: Cameron Freeman

Front Cover Photograph: Andersen Ross/Brand X Pictures

Back Cover Photograph: Lorne Fromer

Distributed by:
NSA/Nina Spencer & Associates
416-588-3334
nina@ninaspencer.com
www.ninaspencer.com

Printed and Bound in Canada
Transcontinental Metrolitho Book Group

Dedication

In memory of Beryl Miseldine Spencer,

...my dear "mummy", who was always my biggest cheerleader and the most passionate booklover I've ever known.

The world will never be happy until all men have the souls of artists–I mean when they take pleasure in their jobs. — Auguste Rodin

The real voyage of discovery consists not necessarily in seeking new landscapes but seeing with new eyes. — Marcel Proust

Table of Contents

Passion is a choice. Don't be dead from the neck up. Trust your intuition. Know your professional self-worth. Choice. Easier said than done? S.E.E.ing. Change and passion paralysis. Learn to surf. Do something different. Make it stick. Overview of eight passion points to keep loving your living...come what may.

Voice intonation awareness. Give yourself a second chance. Positive thinking, language and word choices. Love your job and never work again. Thank goodness it's Friday. Beating the Monday morning blues. Love it, leave it, change it or stay and hate it. Reversing limiting beliefs. Turning negatives into positives. Transforming "buts" to "ands". Disagreeing diplomatically.

From "pretty good" to "great". Questions for acknowledging your fine workplace contribution. Think "Me Inc." think. Looking in and out of the Johari Window: the public arena, the mask, the blind spot and the unknown.

Laughing at work. The "mug" you bring to work. The less you laugh, the less you laugh. Go for the laughs. Dealing with the "porcupines" at work. Increasing camaraderie and rapport in team meetings. Taming the tiger to access your humour. What happens when you're fighting mad. The anger cycle and how to sever it.

Big picture purpose, systems thinking and we're all in
this boat together. You're more connected than you
think. Elevating networking effectiveness. Questions
for realizing and growing your network. Reconnecting
with your past. Likeability counts. Giving and receiving
feedback for nurturing relationships. Listening to
others with heart. Examples of poor listening. How
to improve listening.

The end of the beginning. Remembering ways to practice passion for your profession everyday. Easier said
than done? The paradoxical commandments. Life is
change, work is change but passion is optional. Make
your choice. Class starts now!

Acknowledgements

I once met a man who promoted that you could write a book, pretty much on your own, in two weeks! I don't know what kind of book *that* would be, but I do know this...*this* book has been some five years in the making and has taken a dedicated team of fine contributors to pull together and bring to life.

My eternal thanks and love go first to Cameron Freeman, my devoted life partner and unofficial business advisor, strategist and coach for the past 15 years. I owe much of my career success, and this book, to Cam's sometimes gentle and sometimes "hard-nosed" support and constant encouragement. I probably *could* have "done it without him" but, for sure, the experience would've been ten times harder and a lot less exciting. Whatever will I do now that Cameron no longer has to keep on chanting in my ear, "Finish the book...finish the book..."?

My gratitude and deep appreciation also extend to:

Brian Broderson, my editor—the "great eliminator"—for making me look good in print, both years ago while writing monthly columns for Canada's "Training Report" and today, in this, my first book.

Bernard Hellen, Principle of Traffic Marketing + Design, Toronto, for his creative savvy, painstaking attention to detail, friendship and, ultimately, for his beautifully designed cover and text layout.

My darling daughter, Kathryn Stephens, who even at the tender age of three, shared simple and sound "old soul" wisdom and advice for business and life. I couldn't be prouder of the fine young woman she's become and I suspect I'll be heeding her wise words and insights all the rest of my days, too!

Jeff Stephens, for always being a trusted, first-string family touchstone for me, through thick and thin...for always being an empathic supporter of my professional and life choices, and for his rock solid dependability, generosity, understanding and unconditional love.

My dear Auntie Kay, who, although an ocean away, stepped into her big sister's shoes and up to the "motherhood plate" for me upon the passing of my mother. My mum would be touched to know her little sister is now my best cheerleader. I cherish our mother-daughter, yet also friendship-style, relationship more with each passing year, and, because of our without-fail weekly 90-minute chats across "the pond", I also thank goodness for cheap rates to England!

My dearest friends, Dianna (Dyavati) Barrett—one of my best teachers and brightest lights in my life—for nearly 30 years of true-blue friendship and love; Irene Gardiner-Harding, for her loyalty, commitment, sincerity, clarity and level-headed business advice; Dr. Anne Marie Miraglia, my cappuccino bosom buddy, who—thanks to also being my next door neighbour— is always the ready for spontaneous conversation, listening and advice; Judit Lakatos Gladman, my grade six teacher back in 1969, and dear friend today, who not only is a current-day champion of my work, but is also one of the first truly inspirational adults from whom I learned important life lessons; and to Helen Wilkie, for sharing her wisdom about the world of publishing and for always being a professional "ear-on-call".

Gary McCrae, who was the first to recognize my professional speaker potential and plucked me from the corporate rank and file to join his team of in-house organizational development workshop facilitators.

And finally, my thanks to so many people, over so many years, who have booked and attended my keynotes and workshops. Thank-you for your continued kind words of positive experience about my presentations, personal workplace tales to tell, heeding and applying my offered "pearls", subscribing to and sharing my complimentary monthly on-line newsletter, "Working Wisdom", visiting and revisiting my website, and staying in touch through emails, phone calls and writing to me with your questions, suggestions and feedback. What a *pleasure and honour* it is to have been of service to you thus far. Until we meet again another day, it's my heart's desire that you find this book educational, inspirational and entertaining.

Introduction

Passion is a Choice

*Make your choice adventurous stranger. Strike the bell
and bide the danger, or wonder til it drives you mad...
what would have followed if you had.*— C. S. Lewis

Are *you* passionate about your profession? Did you used to
be, but not lately? Perhaps not for a long while? How do you feel
about your work?

If you're *not* passionate about your profession...why not?
What does your lack of passion cost you personally and professionally? Does it affect the quality and satisfaction of your
day-to-day work contribution?

If you hold a leadership position in your organization, does
it affect your experience of the day, your staff, the organization's corporate culture and your bottom line results?

I massage this C.S. Lewis quote (above, from the first in his
Chronicles of Narnia series of children's books, *The Magician's
Nephew*) to dare you to *take a working adventure and feel
passion for your profession* rather than wondering, for the rest
of your days, what it would have been like to have loved your
job and the organization for which you worked.

Too many people opt for the latter. You can test this out
yourself. The next time you're at a cocktail party, forgo the
usual, "So what do you *do* for a living?", for this:

"If you won the nation's biggest lottery, what would you do?"

Most people will tell you, "I'd quit my job, for starters!" OK,
but *after* you've quit, bought everything you always wanted,
visited all the places you always wanted to see, helped all your
friends and family and given to all your favourite charities and
causes—when you're *still* stuck with a gazillion left over
dollars—when you get tired of living in the lap of luxury and
doing nothing and you declare, "I want to go back to work!",
what then?

"That would never happen," you say? Why does this seem

so implausible? Over the years I've known *four* people who won retirement-style lottery jackpots and eventually went back to work. Even Oprah Winfrey has a job; even Bill Gates goes to work.

To what job would *you* return? If you had no need to stay in the job you have, what would you do?

Don't Be Dead From the Neck Up!

Those who follow their hearts seldom lose their way.
— Anonymous

I once spoke at a conference alongside Dr. Margaret Wheatley, a respected American author on business leadership. Since my keynote, *Getting Passion Out of Your Profession*, immediately followed, I was delighted that she shared her experience working with a particular team over several days. No matter what processes she facilitated and no matter how she tried, one young man was, "dead from the neck up." On Friday, he volunteered to take Dr. Wheatley to the airport. He was animated and chatty and full of exuberance. Dr. Wheatley was flabbergasted at his shift in energy. She asked him why he was so excited. The answer: because on Saturdays and Sundays he taught aerial acrobatics!

That was his passion! *That* was the line of work he should have pursued. Did he bother exploring how to make it happen? What do you think?

I know what you're thinking: "It's nice to say that we should quit our day jobs and follow our bliss, but I have a house and a family and all kinds of reasons to stick with my job."

I remember a line in a popular song from the '70s: "If you can't be with the one you love, honey, love the one you're with." Do you know this song? I'm not going to ask you to stop reading and break into a chorus, but consider the message of this lyric (with a little spin on it). If you can't be in the *job* you'd love, honey, love the job you're in! Love the job you're in.

That might be a little bit easier said than done, but you *can* consciously decide to have passion for your job while working towards your dream. Passion doesn't just come to us by accident, or fall on us like fairy dust—*we* make it happen. *You* make it happen! And it all starts with your thinking.

Wherever you go, go with all your heart. — Confucius

I've contributed two decades to the discipline of organizational development and conference keynoting, including my early years in a large organization. Several years before I chose to leave corporate life, I started subscribing to the thinking, "This organization may not be the ultimate vehicle for contributing to my profession in organizational development, but I've chosen to stay put for now, for whatever reasons, so I'm going to love the job I'm in, for the time being."

Trust Your Intuition

Intuition is perception via the unconscious.
— Carl Jung

One spring day, while I was still with that organization, I travelled to Hamilton, Ontario (just 45 minutes down the road from my home in Toronto), to facilitate a change management workshop. My dear mother was to have a few days "sleep over" with my family starting that evening, and I'd previously arranged to pick her up at day's end. I called her several times the night before and again during workshop breaks to remind her of our plans. Each time there was no answer. I started to worry and shared my fret with the managers in the workshop; they kindly agreed to cut the day short so I could make sure all was right.

Well, it wasn't all right...it was *all wrong!*

I continued calling my mother while driving back to Toronto, but there was still no answer. I had a sinking, dreadful feeling that something terrible had happened. And so I called Bruno, the superintendent of her building, and asked him to check in on her.

About 10 minutes later, while still enroute, Bruno called

back, bumbled and stumbled over his words, and finally said, "I think your mom is dead." Even though on some level I may have known what Bruno was going to say, consciously, I was completely unprepared. My mother was only 68 years old. She loved her life, she had passion, she lived alone but wasn't lonely and she was healthy. There was nothing wrong with her! But she was dead.

Intuition is a spiritual faculty and does not explain, but simply points the way. — Florence Scovel Shinn

My mother's passing must have led to some subconscious soul-searching about my own direction in life. Two days later, just before friends and family came to pay respects on the night before the funeral, as I sat quietly, mustering my stiff upper lip, I blurted out to my husband, "That's it! I'm quitting my job."

The moment before I said it, I didn't know I was going to say it. We both sat quietly, letting this declaration sink in; never had anything been so clear and felt so right for me, in my entire life. It was a magical moment I'll vividly remember forever.

I started telling some of my inner circle of friends and colleagues about my exciting news—only those I thought would be kind and supportive of my decision. Their reactions weren't what I expected: "What are you going to do for a living? Nina it's grief—*don't do it*. You know you're really reactive and vulnerable right now. Take it slowly. What about all your years of *seniority*? What about your *pension*?"

Talk about killjoys.

But their worries seeped into my consciousness and I thought, "Maybe they're right. I'll give it six months. And, if in six months I still feel this way, I'm outta here!"

Intuition is reason in a hurry. — Holbrook Jackson

I couldn't shake the feeling it was time to move on. I loved my work in corporate organizational development, and I still loved doing it for the organization I served, but my decision to leave wasn't about running *away* from my corporate job—it was about moving *towards* something new. Something next.

By the autumn of that same year I *knew* I would leave, and so I did, during the first week of December, on my birthday.

Was I scared to leave after so many years with one employer? Strangely to some, I wasn't scared a bit.

Know Your Professional Self-Worth

Intuition will tell the thinking mind where to look next. — Jonas Salk

Through the years I listened and counselled so many individuals who approached me during workshop breaks, sharing their secret fears about their professional worthiness. Classic worries they whispered to me, time and time again, included, "If I get downsized, laid off or declared redundant, who else out there is going to hire me? Where else will I find this level of work, with the kind of salary to which I've become accustomed? I'm a victim of the 'golden handcuffs' and I don't know if anybody else would want my professional services!"

My heart would ache for them because I knew they really believed that no one else would *ever* hire them. Where was their sense of self-esteem? How had they lost their professional self-confidence? We can all appreciate how intimidating it is to update your resume and shop yourself around, especially if you've been with one employer for over a decade. Especially if you had the kind of position, perhaps for years, in which *you* were the one in the recruitment and selection chair. There's definitely, for most, an indirect correlation between years of service with one company and professional self-confidence on the open market.

My philosophy, in a nutshell, was (and is), if you were really no good *here*, then you'll be no good *there*; others will know it and you'll have a hard time. But if you really *were* good here, then you'll be terrific somewhere else, too; someone else, somewhere else will see your value, even if it takes a little time to find something new. Persevere, believe in yourself and your gifts, talents, skills and competencies, and listen to your intuition.

Until one is committed, there is hesitancy, the chance to draw back, always ineffectiveness. Concerning all acts of initiative and creation, there is one elementary truth the ignorance of which kills countless ideas and splendid plans: that the moment one definitely commits oneself, then providence moves too. All sorts of things occur to help one that would never otherwise have occurred. A whole stream of events issues from the decision, raising in one's favor all manner of unforeseen incidents, meetings and material assistance which no man could have dreamed would have come his way. Whatever you can do or dream you can, begin it. Boldness has genius, power and magic in it. Begin it now. — W.H. Murray and Goethe

Think, right now, of someone you know who was initially devastated to lose their coveted job due to a downsizing, or some similar reason—someone who held a respected position within one company for many years. Maybe they had a tough time when it first happened but, in the vast majority of cases, a year or two later, they probably told you, *"It was the best thing that ever happened to me!"* Right?

Knowing your professional self-worth makes all the difference. *Knowing* this accelerates your passion for your profession...and *knowing* has everything to do with your thinking and self-talk. What do *you* say to yourself about your daily work experience and contribution? How are *you* thinking and feeling about your day-to-day professional worth?

On the days leading up to my exit, I was overwhelmed at the number of colleagues who took the time to express their farewells. What do you think so many of them said? "You're so lucky! I really admire you. I wish I had the courage to quit." To listen to their wistfulness, you'd think I was being parolled from a lengthy prison sentence, and that *their* parole had been denied! "Someday I'll quit, too, and start my own business...but not right now", many revealed. I knew on the day *I* left that my colleagues were, at least in large part, dewy eyed because they wished it were them, not me, going.

Choice

*It is almost impossible for anyone, even the most inef-
fective among us, to continue to choose misery after
becoming aware that it is a choice.* — William Glasser

My point isn't that to find your professional passion, you
must quit your job. What I *am* saying is that it's an amazing
and crying shame that so many people would rather be somewhere other than in their current job. For some, it's not that
they don't like the organization they work for or their profession, it's just that they're stressed out or bored to death. Either
way, whatever love they once felt for their work is now an echo-
ing memory rather than a current reality. If I conducted a
roving reporter survey at lunchtime in any downtown business
core, asking, "Have you ever entertained the idea of quitting
your job and leaving your current profession?" what do you
suppose the answer would be? I suspect that a lot of people
would say, "Yes, I've thought about it...almost daily!"

You don't have to quit your job to have passion for your
profession, but if you do want to feel more passion for the good
work you perform, consciously *decide* to get clear about how
you want to experience your workdays. Passion for any job,
from the most modest of frontline positions to the loftiest executive suites, is a *choice*. If you decide to demonstrate gusto,
energy, enthusiasm and passion for whatever job you're
performing, you *will* gain it! Even if you have to "fake it 'til you
make it" for a while, you'll still reap the same rewards from your
demonstrated, impassioned outlook and behaviour.

Did I Hear You Say, "Easier Said Than Done"?

*Passion is energy. Feel the power that comes from
focusing on what excites you.* — Oprah Winfrey

The expression, "easier said than done," has been around
for a long time. Erase it from your vocabulary. It's a classic
excuse for not even bothering to try. Here's a replacement:

"Just do it." Just *choose* to be passionate about your work.

When I hear people say, "Easier said than done", while arguing why they'd rather stay put, even if they're miserable, I think of two inspiring passages. The first is from author, Richard Bach's 1970's classic, *Jonathan Livingston Seagull:* "When you argue for your limitations, you get to keep them". The second is from regarded author and speaker Brian Tracy: "Anything worth doing well is worth doing poorly at first".

Intellectually, we may see the benefits of adopting a different approach, but habit keeps us stuck in old patterns of thinking and doing. Most of us won't change until we get a whack on the side of the head to wake us up. Something has to *happen.* So you lose a parent, or you get downsized, or you get fired or you survive a serious illness. Some sort of significant emotional event happens that gives you a bop on the side of the head and makes you say, "From this point on I'm going to put more daily passion and zeal into everything I do, including my work, because life can be so unpredictable and there's no time to waste on the trivial and the negative." Isn't it amazing that so many of us have to experience some kind of physical or mental pain and suffering before we "giddy up" and change our ways? We don't really have to wait for metaphoric or literal pain to shift to a more positive outlook. We can consciously decide that there really is no time like the present to make the passion shift.

SEEing

Isn't it a lovely and even mildly profound, coincidence that, "Significant Emotional Event", makes the acronym S.E.E.? It often takes a "SEEing" to *see* the truth about which way to go next. Another name for a "SEEing" is CBK. ...Cosmic Butt Kick! Who needs a CBK? Anyone you know? Yourself perhaps? A CBK works like this: The universe says, "I'm going to give you this experience; are you going to *get* it?" If you say, "No!", and don't get it, you get another CBK another day! And then you get another, and another, and another, until you *finally* say, "OK, OK. Enough already! I get it!" The "eureka" is born and new action follows.

Change and Passion Paralysis

In life, change is inevitable. In business, change is vital.
— Warren Bennis

What choices do you make for yourself? Have you ever wondered how things would be if only you'd made different choices? Most of us have. But here we are in this reality making the best of what's in front of us. Can we make it better? Do we *want* to make it better? *How* can we make it better?

Change is everywhere around us. It always has been, but we only started to make it a topic of workplace conversation when things *really* started speeding up. There's been more technological change in this past half century than in the entire recorded history of mankind. In your lifetime, you've been dealing with a phenomenal amount of change while growing up, graduating from school, finding your first job, life partner and perhaps starting a family. Who noticed? But then...bop! A whack on the side of the head came at you, seemingly from nowhere, and shook the normal rhythm of your world. What was that "bop" for you? Do you remember? How did you deal with it? *Did* you deal with it? How has your bop impacted what happened next for you?

How we deal with change has everything to do with how we experience the world around us, at work and elsewhere. To begin my conference keynotes or workshops I often test participants regarding their subconscious attitudes and behaviours towards change by daring them to take my classic 15 second name writing challenge. Although this test appears somewhat silly, and purely for the fun of an opening/icebreaker-style exercise, for many this experience is a profound bop on the side of the head! A little bit of duping is required to elicit the insightful result, but participant response and insights are amazing, and the groans and moans of new awareness brought on by this challenge are quite audible, too.

When I conduct this test with hundreds of people in a conference setting you can imagine how those individual groans, moans and "aha!" reactions and noises are amplified. Many instinctively compare their personal results with those around them, but I assure all that the good news is, "You're not in competition with the person to your left or right, in front or behind. It's merely about knowing "where *you're* at"; it's about establishing a standard—a point of reference—from which to reflect and possibly shift your thinking towards change.

If we really want to elevate our passion, or get better at anything at work or in life, we need to know the truth of "where we're at". We need to be able to establish a current standard so that we know what we're shooting for if we wish to go higher or move along.

> *The world hates change, yet it is the only thing that has brought progress.* — Charles Kettering

Yes, it's true. I play a trick on my audiences to get them to see the metaphoric light about their *real* attitudes and behaviours towards change. And isn't that *exactly* what happens in our lives? Isn't that *exactly* what happens at work? We're going along just fine, thank-you very much, doing our work in the same comfortable and confident way we've done for years (or at least for some time), and then someone or something comes along and metaphorically yells, "CHANGE!" (which often feels like a nasty and unkind trick). The change happens, whether we're ready or not, whether we like it or not, and things never return to the old way ever again. Some roll with it and love it; some are frozen in the headlights (at least for a while); and some stubbornly play ostrich for as long as possible.

> *Employees don't resist change, they resist being changed.* — Peter Scholtes

At work, the "CHANGE!" could be the new broom sweeping of a new CEO, director, or some other adjustment in the corporate organizational structure. The "CHANGE!" could be a new policy or procedure, a merger or acquisition, a downsizing, a new piece of software or new technology to do the same old job—it's anything that shakes up your work world. In private life, it could be a move to a new home, or new city, or even a new country. It could be a new primary relationship, or the pain of the ending of one, a new family member, the death of a loved one or the diagnosis of a serious personal injury or illness. Each of us deals with change in our own way. The way participants individually respond to my silly little keynote opening writing exercise often eerily parallels the way we respond to actual changes that occur in our lives. Do we ride the waves of change or get doused by them? How about you?

Learn to Surf

So much has been written about employees' resistance to change that we are sometimes tempted to forget that they can also react favourably.
— Nathaniel Stewart

Author Jack Kornfield once quoted, "You can't stop the waves, but you can learn to surf!" What he meant was, the waves of change will keep coming no matter what, just like the ocean tides. The only thing we *can* do is become adept at handling them. Learning to "surf" is a prerequisite to increasing passion for your profession.

Many of us react to change in crisis mode, whether we chose the change ourselves or it was thrust upon us. It's interesting to note that the Chinese word for "crisis" translates literally into English as both "threat" and "opportunity". Like the Chinese word for "crisis" suggests, we can learn to see change as a threat to our way of life, or we can reach inside and consider how the change offers personal opportunity. Typically, when we embrace the change, we see its benefits, but when we think it's not in our best interest, it seems threatening. The trick is to practice positive self-talk so that, even in situations where we know we are "knee jerking" with panic and fear, we ask ourselves what's good about the situation and what lesson can we draw from it.

Some changes present an honest to goodness threat worth fighting but, in our personal lives, and at work, so many of us so often react by feeling threatened that we don't spend *even one moment* considering WIIFM? And *that's* not an American radio station—it's "What's In It For Me?" "What's in it for *me* to ignore my feelings of threat so that I can have a few moments to ponder how this scary change may be an *opportunity* from which I can learn or benefit?"

Every now and then I hear an audience member say, "Nice idea in theory, but I'm too old to change. You can't teach an old dog new tricks...and *I'm* an old dog!" This declaration always reminds me of a wonderful Gary Larson comic, which so succinctly captures this participant's feeling. Picture this: a dog on a unicycle, on a high wire, with a cat in its mouth and a vase balanced on its nose, juggling and hoola-hooping, with a crowd of people watching in the stands. The caption reads, "High above the hushed crowd, Rex tries to remain focused. Still, he can't shake one nagging thought...he is an old dog and this is a new trick."

Old dogs and new tricks. Have you ever felt like that? "I'm an old dog. I don't want to learn any more new tricks! Can't I keep applying the old policies and procedures that we've used and practiced for years? Can't I keep doing my job the old way? The way I already know how? Can't things just stay the same until I retire? I only have five (or ten, or fifteen) years to go!"

Many people stereotype the "old dogs" as employees over forty. Are you over forty? So many of us automatically assume that if *anyone* is going to give us (or the organization) grief over a grand or even insignificant little change, it's going to be "the old" guys over forty! In the workplace, these are the people who can remember black telephones that rang off the wall until someone answered them, the one computer per team, (or floor!), messy ditto copying machines (requiring carbon paper—if you don't know what I'm talking about here, just ask someone over forty!), and the sound of typewriters clicking away, while "secretaries" stuffed little pink papers into plastic round cubbyhole molds, name-labeled with Dymo-tape, for managers and others to pick up their telephone messages upon return from their meetings, lunch or whatever. It's true, there are some people in the workplace who do have a great deal of seniority and have difficulty surfing the waves of change. Equally true, however, is the fact that there are plenty of others in our work world who are under 30, already exhibiting blatant signs of being "old dogs". We need to be careful with our stereotypes and anticipations of who among us is going to have difficulty, or give us the greatest amount of grief, over change, workplace or otherwise.

Cultural anthropologist Jennifer James reminds us that, as individuals in the workplace of the 21st century, we're working with essentially the same brains that our ancestors possessed two or three hundred years ago. James points out that there is more stimulus coming at us in our morning commute to our workplaces than a farmer faced, two or three hundred years ago, in an entire month! So if you secretly think that you don't know whether you're coming or going on some days, or if you can't always remember the names of your own family members, or you can't remember the name of your boss (and you've been working with that person for years!), the good news is...you're not going crazy! Whew! What a relief to know! This is normal for the times. You've got a lot on your plate at all times and a lot coming at you on any given day.

> *Smart organizations of the future won't try to manage change processes. Instead they will nurture the spirit of change within their people. That way, change will occur naturally and will preserve the heart and soul of the organization.* — Sue Simmons

Accepting the craziness of the world, and the pace of it, as "normal" doesn't necessarily help add sanity to our days, but there are strategies, techniques and skills that can help us be peaceful, focused, and passionate on the inside, no matter what changes are happening on the outside. A commitment to practicing these techniques daily will take us from surviving to thriving, and help us rekindle the original passion we felt for our profession, come what may.

Do Something Different

> *If you always do what you've always done, you'll always get what you've always got.* —Anonymous

In 1990, I came across a saying that's become one of my all time favourites: "If you always do what you've always done... you'll always get what you've always got!" I regret that I'm not sure who first said it, but this much I do know: anytime I'm frustrated over a recurring, dissatisfying result, I hear that saying in my head and ask, "Well, Nina, if you want to get something different, you've got to *do* something differently! What's it going to be?"

A few years ago my family had the use of a friend's cottage for a week. Being city slickers this was a welcome change. None of us had our own fishing rods but my children knew they'd want to "go fishin'" so I rummaged around the back of the garage for some old fishing rods I'd had as a pre-teen (which was 30 years ago!). Somehow, I found them. Through my rose-coloured, nostalgic glasses, I declared that the rods were "like new." In reality, they were arthritic and enjoying their dusty, rusty neglected retirement.

Within moments of arriving at the cottage, the kids dug out my old rods from the bottom of the trunk, and prepared them for their first casts. The rods didn't work. No matter how hard they tried, these rods had gone kaput—small wonder! Braving my children's long faces (and now knowing that I should've passed on "memory lane" and just bought new rods before we left the city), I said, "Never mind. First thing tomorrow, I'll go into town and buy brand new rods." That pleased them well enough and, with that, they turned around and went swimming instead.

But my husband! Could *he* leave it at that? Absolutely not! For the best part of the next hour he tried and tried and tried to make those rods work! He eventually surrendered to my good judgment and said, "OK, I give up. Let's get new rods first thing tomorrow!" Now, hey...*there* was a good idea! Why didn't *I* think of that??? Later that evening, at twilight, when the bugs were upon the water and the fish were jumping with delight at the abundance of their feed, my husband rushed down to the dock, grabbed for those poor old tired rods and once again *commanded* that they work! When they refused, and after he had hooked himself with an aborted cast, the cursing in comic strip fashion began, "#@!!#!!@##!" Never have I had a more classic example from my own experience (or my husband's) that so richly demonstrated, "If you always do what you've always done, you'll always get what you've always got!" If you want to get something different you've got to DO SOMETHING DIFFERENT! You want to catch some "fish"? Get a new rod!

Make it Stick

After all the layoffs, early retirements, reengineering and restructuring, what is the glue that will hold this organization together? — David Noer, *Breaking Free*

The work world (and all of the world for that matter) is in a state of transition. No kidding! At work, especially, things are changing at a faster pace than ever before. As cliché as that truth is fast becoming, we know it to be so, like it or not. And this transition will probably last all the rest of our work lives and beyond. This may not be news but it's still a big adjustment for people who have been in their jobs long enough to remember a different way, but not long enough to yet retire. Major forces contributing to change in the workplace include cost pressures, downsizing, restructuring, mergers and acquisitions, rising client demands, social changes, shifting values, automation, information technology, to travel or not to travel, and issues of national security. Have I left anything out? Oh yes, social and physical global uncertainty, too! Many people believe these changes are a threat to their sense of comfort, success and satisfaction and are having a hard time seeing their way around it while trying to continue living and working in their own backyards.

No matter what your job, whether it's in the work world or in the home, for a deeper sense of personal satisfaction and success, it's valuable and important to develop increasingly higher levels of self-awareness, self-management, interpersonal communications and respect for self and others, and to periodically remind yourself about why you loved performing your chosen work, in the first place.

What *is* the glue that's going to keep us afloat in our day-to-day professional and personal lives? How *can* we find deeper meaning in our work, and inspiration from our daily contributions, in the face of the stresses and challenges of our new workplace reality?

In the balance of this book, I'll share eight kinds of "glue" for helping you do more than just survive at work and elsewhere in the days ahead. Development and maintenance of these skills and perspectives will help you thrive and bolster your sense of confidence to deal with any situation that comes your way. Becoming a practicing student of these strategies, all the rest of your days, will help you reclaim your early days passion for your profession and give you the mettle to ride out even your darkest hours of doubt about your chosen field of work.

Some people have more confidence, focus and energy than others to fortify themselves in topsy-turvy times. Some people are naturally wired to sustain passion for their profession through all their working years, no matter what. For others, it's not always that easy.

To bring that confidence to life for yourself, to reconnect with passion for your profession (or to sustain it), and keep it in a holding pattern forever more, embrace and practice these eight passion points:

1. **Practice Positive Thinking and Word Choice:**
   Consciously choose positive language and thinking to influence your passion for your work, and to inspire the passion of others.

2. **Project Professional Self-Worth:**
   To really get a hit of the fine contribution you make, be willing to acknowledge, to yourself and others, how well you do what you do.

3. **Protect Sense of Humour:**
   The benefits of keeping your sense of humour are good for both your health and your spirit. Guard against the dreaded and humourless diseases of Psychosclerosis (Hardening of the Thinking) and HDS (Humour Deficiency Syndrome) that slip into workplace settings and zap everyone's chances for feeling passion for their professions. Be the one who starts the humour cycle, instead of the anger cycle.

4. **Play with Perspective:**
   Perspective has everything to do with how you think about control. What do you control? What don't you control? Who do you control? Who don't you control? Think of control like the weather: when you go outside you get whatever's there! It's up to you to modify your perspective so that you can deal with all the workplace "weather" successfully.

5. **Profess Your Purpose:**
   It's easier to stay the course when you know deeply why you're doing what you're doing. Getting clear about your bigger purpose helps. Try the "five whys" test. Ask yourself, five times, "Why do I do this job?" and for each answer, ask, "And why is that important to me?" By the fifth "Why" you'll be getting closer to the truth of your pure purpose for doing the good work you perform.

6. **Preserve Energy and Enthusiasm:**
   Energy is the groundwork for enthusiasm and the only thing more contagious than enthusiasm is...the *lack* of it. Practice daily strategies for taking care of your physical and emotional energy.

7. **Promise to Persevere:**
   You may be in the right job for you, and in the right organization, too, but still get into a funk about work from time-to-time. In those cases, cut yourself some slack and persevere. Blue periods usually disappear sooner or later. Learn to keep the faith. Make a list of the things that you really love about your work (and then keep that list close by to look at every now and then).

8. **Perpetuate Relationships:**
   Find creative, time-efficient ways to stay in touch with your circle of influence and expand that circle regularly. Sincerely and authentically network your guts out. Keep in touch with enthusiastic, energized colleagues in your field, as well as outside your field, to help sustain your passion for your profession. Be sure to attend and champion employer-supported internal conferences, and attend some external ones, such as professional association conferences, too!

Association conferences and in-house, formal professional developmental workshops can make a big difference in what happens next in your career or life.

> *When you're green you're growing; when you're ripe you rot.* — Anonymous

Take a careful look at this list of eight passion points. Who do you know who embraces and demonstrates *all* of these skills? To which do you find yourself saying, "I already do that one"? To which do you instinctively know, "There's room for improvement for me with this one"?

You're probably already a walking, talking positive example of at least some of these skills, and it's your competency with these skills that's helping you surf the waves of change and uncertainty so far. How much better can you get? How much better do you think you'll *need* to get? Remember, "When you're green you're growing, and when you're ripe, you rot!" You can never get too good at the skills that are essential for thriving at work and in your personal life.

The rest of this book will explore each of these eight passion points. You may choose to read sequentially, from cover-to-cover if you like, or if you prefer, visit the chapters that speak to you most, first. Whatever your preferred reading style or strategy, it's my desire that, at the very least, you're reminded of things you already know but have put on the back burner. Or, at most, I cause you to have one (or many) of those lovely "Aha" life-changing experiences that I affectionately referred to earlier as CBK's (Cosmic Butt Kicks, remember this?).

When these momentous occasions occur, they can inspire us to take immediate action to do things differently, or think differently, all the rest of our days. These whacks on the side of the head create the exhilarating SEEings most of us wish would appear more often. So, if by chance or good fortune, this book comes to you at just the right time (in the Zen fashion of, "When the student is ready the teacher appears"), and you *do* have one or more SEEings, I'd be delighted to hear from you! It's always fun to share the celebration of the "eureka" with an appreciating other. My contact information is at the back of this book.

1

Passion Point #1:
Practice Positive Thinking and Word Choice

The more a man meditates upon good thoughts, the better will be his world and the world at large.
— Confucius

Look in any newspaper's career section, or on the web, for qualifications and requirements of *any* advertised job these days. What do they all say about interpersonal communication skills? "Must have _____ interpersonal communication skills". Do they say "good"? Maybe. More times than not, however, they insist on "excellent" skills. Everyone says they have these skills yet we all know of at least one or two people at work who don't seem to have any! We find ourselves asking, "How *ever* did they get hired??? Whom did they *fool* in their interview?" Yes, it's true that some people have achieved quite a lot in positional power with quite a *little* in the people skills department. No one seemed to think that they were in need of any official guidance or education in interpersonal communications.

In a world of rapid change and increasing interdependence, learning is too important to be left to chance.
— Peter Senge, *The Fifth Discipline Fieldbook: Strategies and tools for building a learning organization*

Historically, people were promoted based on their technical competency at performing their current job. For this they received a promotion, and perhaps some technical training, but interpersonal communications learning was left to chance. Even if these people sincerely wanted to be more effective communicators, for the most part, they were left on their own to figure it out. It's only in recent years that the best of employers have realized the need to make sure that people in leadership positions receive *formal* learning opportunities in interpersonal communications. The old adage is so true, "Manage things. Lead people".

The subject of interpersonal communications is huge; volumes have been written. When I ask my audiences to consider their own competency with interpersonal communications, I ask them to particularly focus on assertive communications, conflict resolution, and especially on positive thinking, positive word choice and the actual sound of it all.

Voice Intonation Awareness

> *Mend your speech a little, lest it may mar your*
> *fortunes.* — William Shakespeare, *"King Lear"*

UCLA psychology professors Albert Mehrabian and J. A. Russell documented some interesting interpersonal communication statistics in their 1974 book, *An Approach to Environmental Psychology*. After conducting a controlled study, they reported that 55% of face-to-face communications is transmitted through body language, 38% through tone of voice, and 7% through the actual words we choose. Ever since then, countless speakers and organizational development workshop facilitators have grabbed, massaged and manipulated these statistics to illustrate their own points about face-to-face interpersonal communications. Some of my colleagues are very cynical that this information is still making the rounds over thirty years later. Touché! Amazingly though, there are still thousands upon thousands of people who've never heard these figures.

These statistics haven't taken into consideration the tremendous amount of change in our world in the past 35 years. An updated study may very well yield somewhat different results. But this much is true...*some* percentage of face-to-face communications will always be communicated through body language (as long as you're in a body), tone of voice and word choice. And they're *all* important to the final result—the message perceived and received by another.

Since so much of our communication occurs over the phone, or via email, it's important to pump up our awareness of tone and word choice. Everyone knows how to read body language, at least to a certain extent, even if they've never read a book or attended a workshop on the subject. We all come wired to understand and interpret the communication of body language—that's why we don't bump into each other in the streets (well, at least most of the time). And have you noticed that when you *do* have those occasional awkward moments of dancing the cha-cha shuffle with a stranger, in a hall or on the street, it's because one of you had your head down, so you couldn't "read" the other? The same can also be said of tone. You know how the saying goes, "It's not what you said...it's how you said it."

> *In the right key anything can be said. In the wrong key, nothing. The only delicate part is in the establishment of the key.* — George Bernard Shaw

There are definitely ways to experiment with the truth of this declaration in the workplace, but we can also test this hypothesis in home life. My dog (a beautiful Soft-Coated Wheaten Terrier named Angus) loves car rides but hates going to the veterinarian—quite typical. All I have to say, in a gleeful, excited voice is, "Angus ... do you want to go for a car ride, to go to the vet's, to get a big needle?" and he goes crazy, prancing around the house looking for his lead, then promptly standing by the door, barking with delight as he impatiently waits for me to hurry up. It doesn't matter to him, at all, that I've mentioned the vet and a big needle. He was "so there" with the mere tone of my voice as I gushed those first few words declaring I was going somewhere and *he* was invited! Now I'm not trying to suggest that people are like dogs...following you anywhere if you'd only use the right tone of voice, but I *am* suggesting that whether it's a furry friend or a hairy client, tone of voice can make a big difference in the responses and results you get.

Try this simple test. It's one of those tests that works especially well when acted out with others, so, if you *really* want to go the distance with this experiment, rally around a few colleagues, and tell them you're testing your ability to get your intended message across using voice tone.

You'll be saying aloud, this simple sentence: "I didn't say she stole the laptop." With conscious and forceful voice intonation stressed on different words within this sentence, you can create five different meanings. Ask your audience to interpret your intended message as you experiment with voice intonation five times over.

Say this sentence aloud, five times, stressing only the italicized word in each case:

1. **"*I* didn't say she stole the laptop." ...implies someone else said it, not me.
2. "I didn't **say** she stole the laptop." ...suggests I implied it, or hinted at it, instead.
3. "I didn't say **she** stole the laptop."...means *he* stole it; or someone else.
4. "I didn't say she **stole** the laptop."...means she merely borrowed it ... forever!
5. "I didn't say she stole the **laptop**."...suggests she stole something else—the desk top, perhaps?

Are you consciously aware of your own voice tone 100% of the time? Is anyone?

Do you think that some of your business and personal relationships can go off the rails because the other person was offended by your tone? Do you think that, at least in some of those cases, you'd never even know what happened? Is there room in your life to put more thoughtful and conscious energy into the tone of what comes out of your mouth? It's not about denying your natural way of being; it's about becoming a master of interpersonal communications. Listen to *how* you put across *what* you put across. Even if it comes out "wrong" (and in the next split-second, you know it), you can still fix it. In such a case, tell the receiver of your words that you are consciously working on making your tone match your sincere, desired intent. Ask the receiver to bear with you as you do a rewind and deliver the statement again. Check with the receiver for understanding.

Give Yourself a Second Chance

It is not sufficient to know what one ought to say, but one must also know how to say it. — Aristotle

One of the safest and easiest ways to practice tone of voice is to change your telephone voice mail daily. Also, play back voice mails you leave for business associates, clients and personal contacts before sending the messages on their way. Listen for your intonation. Decide on your intended energy and power level *before* you record the message, then play it back and ask yourself, "If this were a message *I* was receiving, how would I interpret it? How would I interpret the person's energy, manner and urgency? Is it clipped, warm or cold, open or closed? Does it inspire me to call the person back, immediately?" If you play back your message, and you don't like it, or it doesn't come across the way you thought you'd recorded it, erase it and re-record. It may take a few more precious moments but it could save personal relationships and your professional reputation. Most of us sometimes wish we could take back a nasty or irritable voice mail, hastily sent, that resulted in much *more* time on the telephone later, doing damage control. If we'd only done it right the first time.

Try this. Decide you want your daily voice mail greeting to sound as though you're glad the caller phoned you. Pretend your favourite person in the world will be listening to your voice mail greeting. Decide you want the caller to be uplifted by your audible energy and impressed by the warmth and sincerity of your recorded voice. Once you have that vision and that imagined sound in your mind's eye, record it. It helps if you physically smile, with cheeks way up high, as you record your greeting. Use a mirror, or look at a picture of a loved one (or even of your beloved family pet, if you like), as you smile and record your message.

How silly is this, you may ask? Well, remember those statistics that suggested that 55% of our communication is body language? It's that very percentage of communication that is lost over the phone; you have to put across a positive style and energy with a 55% disadvantage! Have you ever thought about why morning radio hosts everywhere have such high, perky energy? Chances are, if you were to sit beside them in the studio, you'd find their energy over-the-top and perhaps even insincere. But it doesn't come across that way to the listening audience. Why? Radio personalities know they *have* to put 130% energy and sunny disposition out there because some significant percentage of their enthusiasm is eaten up by the airwaves and the disadvantage of having no visuals. Whether you believe that tone of voice accounts for 38% of communications or not, take advantage of maximizing the positive impression you can create with your tone. At work, change your voice mail daily to get lots of practice with conscious positive, upbeat intonation.

Consider re-recording your family or personal voice mail, too. When was the last time you did *that*? A colleague of mine is married to a retired police officer; he created the outgoing recorded greeting message on their home phone. They received a fair number of hang-ups and couldn't figure out why. Friends (myself included) finally confessed that his message was so intimidating and gruff that they were more inspired to quickly hang up rather than leave a message at all! Now *she* records the greeting message.

Positive Thinking, Language and Word Choices

A man is but the product of his thoughts; what he thinks, he becomes. — Mahatma Ghandi

When I was a child and, from time-to-time, would feel sorry for myself, I'd take a visit to what author Jim Clemmer ("Growing The Distance", "The Leader's Digest") calls, "Pity City". My mother would do her best to offer encouragement and bolster me up by saying, "You should read Norman Vincent

Peale's *The Power of Positive Thinking.*" I can't say how many times I heard that advice from my mum's lips, from about age six until adulthood. Did I listen to her? No. In typical "kid fashion" I defied that good parental advice, and never *did* read *The Power of Positive Thinking* until I was an adult. Whether or not you've ever read Peale, most people easily agree that he's the grandfather of the popularized, modern version of positive thinking. And, despite one's age, it's never too late to jump on the "band wagon". Or, put positively...there's always time to climb aboard! And, in addition to this very volume, here and now, "The Power of Positive Thinking" is a fine book to fortify yourself.

In contemplating positive thinking as a subject of study, it helps to know a little bit about yet another important champion of this philosophy for living—Martin Seligman. Seligman is a cognitive psychologist, director of clinical training in psychology at the University of Pennsylvania and author of *Learned Optimism,* an important work in the self-help field because it provides a scientific foundation for many of its claims. Seligman examines the effects of pessimism and optimism on one's view and experience of life. One of the main premises of his book, based on more than twenty years of research, is that a more optimistic outlook can be *learned.*

Seligman asks what makes people decide to pick themselves up, dust themselves off and start all over again. He discovered that the ability to bounce back, after all kinds of devastating setbacks, was not an act of willpower but a result of how individuals talk to themselves—how they explain such events to themselves. Optimism is a set of skills that can be learned and must be practiced. Yes, it's true that some people seem to be wired with a positive perspective on just about everything, but any of us can move along the pessimistic to optimistic spectrum if we desire.

Life is about the stories you choose to tell yourself. The way you explain events to yourself is directly related to how you react to them. If you tell yourself that a colleague or situation is a *problem,* and then take action to solve the *problem* ... what do you think you'll experience along the way? You guessed it...the feeling of a *problem!*

On the other hand, if you tell yourself that this colleague, or that situation, is a *challenge*, you open yourself up to a different interpretation of the experience and will probably see a more successful end result. Semantics you say? Maybe. Or maybe not. I believe and teach the concept and skill of training the brain to be three seconds ahead of the tongue—making sure your brain is engaged before you put your mouth in gear. What a concept! Another way to practice this skill is to imagine having an out-of-body experience. Author Wayne Dyer suggests being a "compassionate witness" to your own behaviour, in which you work hard to step out of yourself and observe yourself saying the words you speak and behaving the way you do.

> *Real human freedom is the ability to pause between the events of our lives and choose how we will respond.* — Rollo May

It's a challenge to practice this skill 100% of the time (it's not *hard*...it's a *challenge*—see how this works?). Have you ever blurted out something that you later regretted? In such cases, were you left thinking, "What was I thinking of? If only I'd..." If you had been just a bit ahead of yourself you could have consciously and thoughtfully chosen words that kept the lines of communication open. This is the value of positive thinking as it relates to others. This thoughtful caring works for how you speak to yourself, as well.

That voice you hear in your head, all day long (especially when something particularly annoying or irritating happens) doesn't mean you're crazy—it's self-talk. It can have just as much effect on your performance as the comments of others. If you're already a serious student of positive self-talk, consider how you can improve and develop even greater consistency. If you know that there's room in your self-talk style for more positive, optimistic thinking, the good news is it *can* be done!

Positive self-talk will help you achieve your goals. If you habitually give yourself a steady drip of negative messages, tasks will seem more daunting and insurmountable—it becomes a self-fulfilling prophecy. Murphy's Law—whatever *can* go wrong, *will* go wrong—is a quintessential example of negative self-talk, and is often quoted by grumbling coworkers when it comes to the launching of new workplace initiatives, policies or even new computer systems. *Yhprum's* Law (Murphy's Law in reverse) is the positive thinking retort to Murphy: whatever can go *right,* will go *right!* To which law do *you* subscribe? Do you know? Can those around you tell you better than you can tell yourself? Often times, that's the case.

Love Your Job and Never Work Again

Find something you love to do and you'll never have to work a day in your life. — Harvey Mackay

How many people really *love* what they do for a living? It may be that they love their profession, but not necessarily the way it's currently manifesting. Sometimes something gets in the way of feeling the passion.

Let me take you on a trip down memory lane. Remember the last time you exclaimed, "I got the job!" when *you* were the one selected for the coveted position? There's a strong chance the competition was pretty stiff, right? But they picked *you!* It was a cause for celebration. Who did you call? I bet you remember. How did you celebrate? *What happened?* The first blush of excitement and passion for a new position can easily slip away under daily stress, workplace politics and pressure. Before you knew it, the subtle cycle of negative self-talk was going around and around. You may have heard yourself saying, "To *think* I cried tears of *joy* the day I got this job! I should have had my head examined!"

How do you feel about your work, these days? Is it the same as those early, "Hot dog! I got the job," days? Examine your feelings about your day-to-day work activities and experiences. How do you feel about Mondays? Fridays? Sunday evening at about 6 p.m., when the best part of the weekend hours are behind you? How do you sleep Sunday night? What about waking up on Monday morning (probably to an alarm clock)? Do you jump out of bed, doing a jig down the hall to the bathroom? How do you feel about crossing the workplace threshold on the first day of a new week?

Thank Goodness It's Friday!

Mondays are the potholes in the road of life.
— Tom Wilson

For too many people, Monday is *Doomsday!* Does your 6 o'clock alarm hit you like a bolt of lightening? Or does the whole of Monday morning pass you by in a vague and nauseating blur? Take a survey—what percentage of people would you suspect would say Monday is their least favourite day of the week? How many upbeat, inspirational songs are written about Mondays? Are there any restaurants named *Mondays?* Of course not...who'd go? One gray Friday morning in the winter of 1969 (when I was in Grade 6) my beloved teacher, Miss Lakatos, playfully chalked "TGIF!" in the upper right hand corner of the blackboard and asked us to guess what it stood for. We couldn't guess, so she told us. (Thank Goodness It's Friday!). Miss Lakatos taught us, all those years ago, to celebrate Fridays...and she made it fun! We thought she did it for *us* but, knowing now a little more about the challenges of a teacher's work week than I did when I was 11, Miss Lakatos was probably writing "TGIF!" for her own celebration and sanity—not ours. How you feel about your work has much to do with how you feel about the rhythm of your week.

The majority of heart attacks in men occur between 8 and 9 a.m. on a Monday morning—the beginning of the workweek, reported Max Wyman, in his Vancouver Sun article, back on March 16, 1998. He should know...he was one of them! I had often heard this statistic but had never conducted any research of my own on this subject. At times I was sure it was an urban myth, concocted by some fellow professional speaker to help illustrate a platform point about reducing stress. So before repeating this data, yet again, I enquired with the Heart and Stroke Foundation of Ontario—sure enough, a member of their external relations branch confirmed its truth. I further confirmed this truth with a "Monday morning heart attacks" Google search, which yielded pages and pages of information. These findings are supported by multiple medical studies over many years, and in different countries, of which, one of the most respected is the ALLHAT study (an international, multi-center study funded by the National Heart, Lung and Blood Institute, in cooperation with the Department of Veterans Affairs Cooperative Studies Program, with multiple teams across Canada and the U.S.).

> *Monday, Monday...can't trust that day.*
> — The Mamas and The Papas

Why Monday? Think about your own weekend...if you're single, maybe you "party hearty!" If you're married with children, you probably work hard to blend a frenetic agenda of mundane chores and tasks with quality family time, which may very well include driving the kids here, there and everywhere. You may get up just as early (or perhaps even earlier), but you probably go to bed later. Be honest, haven't there been some Monday mornings when you flopped into your workplace chair, exhaled (for the first time in two days) and said, "I *had* to come back to work today to get a rest!"?

Playing around with your circadian rhythms is a major factor in egging on Monday morning heart attacks. Circadian rhythms are daily cyclical variations of patterns of behaviour or physiological functions in all living beings—even those of the single-celled variety. These are the patterns of activity that occur on a 24-hour cycle, and are important biological regulators in virtually every living creature. In mammals, the internal circadian clock resides in the brain, and sunlight is the cue that rewinds this clock. Psychiatric and medical studies have shown that circadian rhythms are involved in depression, jet lag, drug efficacy, memory and insomnia. This "body clock" manages daily functions such as your core body temperature, hormonal release, cognitive ability, as well as your wakefulness and sleepiness. When your natural rhythms are disrupted, as they usually are on weekends, resulting symptoms may include sleep disorders, fatigue, digestive problems and an inability to concentrate. Is all this enough to scare a person into working seven days a week? I certainly hope not! It may give you cause, however, to pause and examine how shaking up your weekend rhythms, coupled with a sinking dread of the impending

Monday morning, may be bad for your health.

What can you do to help make a more peaceful emotional and biological/physiological transition from Sunday night to Monday morning? This is a good question to ask because the impact of Monday morning blues can be devastating.

Figure out which, if not all, of these suggestions will help you beat the Monday morning blues:

- start early, on Friday afternoon, by clearing and cleaning your desk before leaving for the weekend. Even if you can't complete all of your work, tidy up as much as possible. It'll be easier on your eyes come Monday morning

- think of Sunday night as a "school night"; remember that term from childhood? a terrific opportunity to do something special, that would keep you out too late, was always denied with, "No, darling, it's a school night!"

- go to bed at least 30 minutes before your later-in-the-week bedtime; you know you'll probably slip along the timeline as the days go by, but commit to starting the week off right by going to bed at least a bit earlier than usual; a late Sunday night coupled with an early Monday morning can be a killer...literally!

- lay-off coffee, tea and alcohol on Sunday evening; it will give you a better chance at having a peaceful and deep sleep; as well, lay-off eating after 8 p.m. so when bedtime rolls around your body isn't busy digesting food

- as you drift off to sleep on Sunday night, or as you contemplate getting out of bed in the pre-dawn of Monday morning, count your blessings that you have a job to go to, and be proud of it; no matter how humble or grand, whether it's working from or within the home, in a corporate setting, or anything else in between

- banish old 1960's and 70's music messages from The Mamas and The Papas ("Monday, Monday...can't trust that day"), and The Carpenters ("Rainy days and

Mondays always get me down"); think of some new songs to sing. Try playing your favourite music (for real, or in your head) all the way to work

- periodically skip the newspaper on Monday mornings—although, of course, the paper isn't *filled* with bad and sad news, much of what is reported can rattle you on any given day (especially if you're the type of person who has strong views and opinions on most everything); are you worried that you'll miss something important if you don't read it? Not a chance! If a particular Monday morning newspaper heralds the front-page news of something serious, sad or worrisome enough, someone is bound to tell you, anyway. Have you noticed how most of us love to be the ones to report the bad or shocking news first? It's not just CNN! It doesn't necessarily make one a cynic or dark soul, but it does seem to be human nature to want to be the conduit of shocking or breaking news (just remember your own behaviour, or that of those around you, when you first heard of the 9/11 news, southeast Asia's December, 2004 Tsunami or the London Transit system bombings of the summer of 2005—didn't you pick up the phone, or holler down the stairs to someone right away to tell the news?)

- if your commitments allow, and if you really did go to bed early enough on Sunday night, consider getting into work 20 to 30 minutes earlier than everyone else on Monday morning; there really is a lovely serene atmosphere to many workplace environments when only a few are there

- consider a four-day workweek that goes from Tuesday to Friday (if that option is feasible and available in your workplace)

- pitch the idea of working from home on Mondays

- plan your Monday "to do list" on Sunday evening (all time management workshops espouse that it's more effective and efficient—and sane, too—to come into a plan, rather than come in to plan)

- plan your clothes (men and women, alike, right down to your watch and jewelry), and lay them out, all ready to go, on Sunday night; this might be the mother in me coming out, but this practice will help keep you calmer and more organized on Monday morning; if you must travel on a Monday morning, pack the night before, leaving your suitcase open for last minute items to be tossed in just before you leave

- think of ways to brighten up your Monday morning workstation: how about flowers, a special picture of the week, inspiring quote of the week, a welcoming bowl of Hersey Kisses to share with others, saving a special voice mail message and playing it back when you feel a possible tingle of Monday morning blues coming on

- decide that this is the week you're going to become more aware of saying what you need to say (to yourself and others) in a positive way, no matter what

> *Work is love made visible. And if you cannot work with love but only with distaste, it is better that you should leave your work and sit at the gate of the temple and take alms of those who work with joy.* — Kahlil Gibran

Let's take a closer look at this last bullet. How about starting with our culture's loose language about things we "love", "hate", or "can't stand". Most of us "love" to be melodramatic about the words we use to clearly put across our likes and dislikes. For example, list three things you *hate* about your *work*. Now list six things you *love* about your *profession*. It's all in the focus one chooses. Change the focus and attention from *hate* to *love*, and from *work* to *profession*, and list *twice* as many items in the positive category, and you're on your way to shifting to a more positive focus about your day-to-day professional activities.

Do the extended version of this exercise by listing ten things you really *hate* about your job, then ten more, and then even ten *more*! Force yourself to keep going until you've reach 50, even if you have to *squeeeeeze* the last few "hates" out of your brain. Once you're finished this long "hate" list, read it aloud. Reading it aloud is important because it will allow you the opportunity to really hear yourself. In all probability, long before you're even half way through, you'll find that you're bored and sound like a petty whiner, even to your own ears. Now, rip that list up into tiny pieces, metaphorically and literally destroying all that negative expression, and throw it in the garbage.

Now, do this exercise *again,* but in the positive. List ten things you *love* about your profession, then ten more, and then ten more, all the way to 50. Again, even if it takes some time, or if you have to go into tiny details, you must identify 50 "loves". Next, like last time, read these things you love about your profession aloud, only this time, fold the list up and put it in a safe and easy-to-access place so that you can review it anytime you find yourself saying or thinking, "I can't stand my work/colleague/situation. I hate my work at times, etc."

Sometimes people feel they can't *stand* their work. Actually, they probably *can* stand it—they might not *like* it but they can stand it. If you really can't stand it, you have some tough choices to make:

• Love it,

• Leave it,

• Change it (or, if changing it is beyond your power, change the way you think about it), or,

• Stay and hate it.

"Love it" speaks for itself. "Leave it" is always an option; it's an option many don't wish to entertain because years of emotional and physical commitment to one organization, location, industry or profession can feel very comfortable, familiar and secure. My mum used to say, "Better the devil you know than the devil you don't!" This philosophy is at the crux of why, when faced with choice, many would fantasize about leaving but would never really act on it. Leaving is also unpalatable for many because the professional "golden handcuffs" become very comforting after a while; and there's always that nagging voice in the back of so many people's minds that cries, "What about my seniority? What about my pension? Where else would I get this level of job at my age? Who would want me now...at *this* age?"

So...you don't *love* it, you don't want to *leave* it. What are the other choices? What about changing it? "Changing it" is a terrific option if you have the positional power to do so. It may take more effort and time but, in the end, changing it may be more satisfying than leaving. In many cases, however, individuals may have some ability to influence the change for which they hope, but not the ultimate power to make it happen. If you can't effect the change and if you don't want to leave, change the way you *think* about it. Ask yourself, "How can I reframe my perspective and self-talk so that I can get through this challenging time with a maximum of sanity and serenity?"

The last of the choices—stay and hate it—is a killer. For the most part, this philosophy can, and often does, kill the energy and productivity of an entire team. Everyone knows at least someone for whom this description fits. And what do the rest of us call such colleagues behind their backs? The number one answer— "deadwood". I've also heard such people referred to, unkindly, as, "workplace road kill", because they just lay there, motionless, while everyone else maneuvers around their carcass.

I call these sorts the, "Quit and Stayeds", because these people quietly, either consciously or unconsciously, quit their jobs a long time ago but never bothered to announce it and never bothered to physically leave. Quitting and staying is bad for you and it's bad for coworkers and clients; it's the most potentially damaging of all the choices you can make.

> *If you take pains and learn in order to get a reward, the work will seem hard; but when you work...if you love your work, you will find your reward in that.*
> — Leo Nikolaevich Tolstoy

A UCLA study determined that 90% of the thoughts people had yesterday are the same ones they have today. If this is so, it's easy to know how you talk to yourself...just think what you said to yourself yesterday. Without any new data input or new awareness of why you should change, you're probably talking to yourself the same way today as you did then. Even if you're generally a positive, optimistic, hopeful and forward-looking person, you may very well still use negative language on yourself and others without knowing.

Some limiting beliefs that you may hear yourself (or others) say at work, may include:

- I'm no good at remembering names.

- I hate giving presentations...I'm always worried that I'll forget to say something important.

- Who am I kidding? I won't get that promotion...get that contract, etc.

- I'll never get through all of this work.

- My VP would never give me the nod to attend an out-of-town conference. Why bother even asking?

- This assignment is too difficult. I've never taken on anything like this before. I'll never get the hang of it.

Every time you repeat a limiting or negative belief, you give it more power in your mind. Your mind doesn't know the difference; if you say it is so, it will believe you! In work, as in the rest of your life, what you think is potentially what you create. Question your beliefs. When you catch yourself using negative self-talk, ask, "Is this what I want to create?" Use the power of your imagination to practice in your mind what you really want to happen in your reality. When you hear yourself reiterating a habitual negative thought, step on the brakes. Change the thought in your mind to a positive one. For example:

- "I'm no good at remembering names," becomes, "I'm going to improve my effectiveness at remembering names."

- "I hate giving presentations...I'm always worried that I'll forget to say something important," becomes, "Presentations are periodically part of my job. Preparing well will help me remember everything that I want to say."

- "Who am I kidding? I won't get that promotion", becomes, "I'm taking a chance; there are lots of reasons why I could be the successful candidate for this promotion."

- "I'll never get through all of this work!", becomes, "I'll chip away at all of this work the best I can; eventually I'll finish!"

- "My VP would never give me the nod to attend an out-of-town conference. Why bother even asking?" becomes, "Maybe my VP will give me the nod to attend that out-of-town conference. I'll only know for sure if I ask."

- "This assignment is too difficult for me. I've never taken on anything like this before. I'll never get the hang of it," becomes, "This is quite a challenge. This is the first time I've ever done anything like this. Eventually I'll figure it all out."

I once heard another UCLA study, from the late 1980's, determined that the average one-year-old child hears the word "no" 472 times per day! When I first heard this statistic I thought it must be an exaggeration. It's been quite a few years since I've known, first hand, what goes on with small children, but I had a chance to observe it one hot summer's day a few years ago while sitting on my own front porch.

My neighbour, Tom, was babysitting his 15-month-old grandson, Antonio, for the whole summer. Tom was ever so proud to strut his first grandchild up and down the street each morning, while the sun's heat was still bearable. Tom would feed Antonio his breakfast and lunch on the front porch; Antonio would often nap there, too. When he awoke, they played and giggled. Antonio was always reaching or lunging for something forbidden, or for Tom's glasses or his beard, or whatever. Tom would lovingly and laughingly say, "no". But he didn't just say *one* "no" … he'd say, "No, no, no, Antonio…No, no, no…No, no, no." As I heard the rhythmical repetition of these words it hit me like a ton of bricks—perhaps it's true! Perhaps children of such a delicate age really *do* hear "no" as much as 472 times per day. After all, I'd just heard Tom say it about ten times in less than ten seconds!

Now, I know what you may be thinking: "Nina...it's a good thing that one year olds get told "no" multiple times a day...that way they can live to have a *second* birthday!" Touché! But still, it illustrates an important point. Children, from very young ages, learn what to do by being told what *not* to do.

What you think about comes about. — Anonymous

This is the tale of the self-fulfilling prophecy. What you think about comes about, people say, and it's true. It's more valuable, influential and persuasive to articulate what you want to happen rather than what you don't.

Use words that declare what you *do* want, to the exclusion of what you don't. When I first grasped this philosophy my daughter was about three years old. I was determined to be the best mother I could be, so I decided that I would be conscious of the words I used to give my daughter guidance and direction.

Kathryn loved to walk atop the large cement-framed, raised flower gardens outside our community swimming pool. These oversized raised flower containers stood about two feet tall. The cement casings had a top surface, all around, that was about two feet wide. I'd lift Kathryn up to the flat surface, where she would then strut along like the queen of the castle, pretending she was executing daredevil feats on the skinniest gymnast's balance beam that ever was. I would hold her hand, but she insisted on a light, almost invisible touch, so that she could feel as though she were really doing this on her own. We did this every Saturday, directly after swimming lessons, throughout the autumn and winter and then into the spring. At first, without thinking, and in typical motherly tones, I would tell Kathryn, "Don't fall...don't fall." It quickly occurred to me that, just as with positive word choice in workplace interactions, I could be practicing this same philosophy with my daughter. So I shifted my advice to, "be careful", and was much prouder of myself for that. "Be careful...be careful," became my enlightened motherly mantra for the balance of the swimming season.

By the time the spring came, I guess we had both gotten quite cocky about the routine and about Kathryn's agility and competence to perform these amazing feats. Of course, that's always when things go wrong, isn't it? Well that's exactly what happened to us. One particularly glorious late spring morning, Kathryn was on autopilot as she routinely paraded around those raised flowerbeds. She looked at everything except what she was doing, and, I confess, I must have been doing the same. The next thing we both knew, Kathryn fell right off the end of the wall! Thank goodness, as far as accidents go, this was a small one, but there were tears, two scraped knees, grazed hands, and a little girl's bruised ego (and *my* ego took a bruising, too, as I thought to myself, "How *could* you let such a thing happen while you were standing right beside her, holding her hand?"). As I dried Kathryn's tears and patched her up with a couple of band aids that I fished out of my purse (trying to reestablish myself in my own eyes as a responsible, ever-ready mother), I said, " Kathryn, if you're going to do tricky things you've got to pay attention!" Ah ha! There it was...the motherly advice that went one better than, "Be careful"! "Pay attention!", is what I should've and could've been saying all along. What an evolutionary concept!

From, "don't fall", to "be careful", to "pay attention"; this is an everyday example of the evolution of turning an unconscious and negative thought pattern into a positive one. And, fifteen years later, I'm still the "go to" person for band-aids (old ways die hard, I guess and, after all, I *was* a Brownie and a Girl Guide as a kid, and then, later on, a Girl Guide leader, so I learned my lessons well...always "be prepared"!).

Positive self-talk plays a big part in fortifying your esteem and can yield a higher probability of getting the results you desire when interacting with others (and everyone would like more of that, I'm sure). *Talk* yourself into it. Do you generally use negative or positive language? Do you know? Are you sure? Negative thinking is habitual, subtle and universal, and we all learn it early.

> *Habit is habit, and not to be flung out the window by any man, but to be coaxed down the stairs one step at a time.* — Mark Twain

Look at these classic expressions often heard at work when interacting with colleagues or clients/customers. Do you hear yourself in these sentences? If you are in a leadership position, have you ever heard your staff use these types of sentences with colleagues or clients?

Look for the negative in each of these sentences:

1. I can't do anything about it until I've talked with my VP.
2. You have to complete the required forms.
3. Have I got you at a bad time?
4. You've called the wrong department. You should've called human resources.
5. You've completely missed my point! Or, You've completely misunderstood me!
6. Thank you for holding (or waiting).
7. I think you do a great job but...
8. I'm either away from my desk or on my phone, so please leave a message and I'll try to get back to you as soon as possible.
9. I'm sorry it's taken me so long to get back to you but I've been so busy, and it's been crazy around here, and I was on vacation, too.
10. If you have any questions, please don't hesitate to call.

Here's how to positively turn each of these sentences around:

Negative Sentence #1:
"I can't do anything about it until I've talked to my VP."

This suggests nothing is going to happen until I've had a conversation with the person to whom I report. You can almost hear the tires screeching to a halt and you know that the person on the receiving end of this declaration will probably *not* be pleased.

"I can't" and "until" are the negative backbone words of this sentence. They slam on the brakes and may cause some momentary strain between you and the person on the receiving end of this statement. Keep the essence of this message and make it positive by taking out "I can't". No one wants to hear that statement in response to his or her expressed needs.

Everyone would much rather hear what *can* and *will* be done. So here's the positive reworking of this sentence, "I *can* do something (or, I'll know what I can do) once I've talked with my VP."

The message is still the same—everything is on hold until the representative has spoken with the VP. The difference is tone and words. Saying what you can't do until...creates a wall between you and the listener, who may interpret your negative sentence as a declaration that you wish to wash your hands of responsibility for action. When you choose to declare what you *can* do *when*, you subtly let the listener know that you're on the case, willing to take action and ultimately are still on his or her side. In this case, choosing the positive alternative sentence structure for this message shows the receiver that you're pointing the way ahead, rather than throwing up roadblocks. This can make a difference in how you and this other individual relate to each other in the days, weeks and months ahead. Perception is everything!

Negative Sentence #2:
"You have to complete the required forms."

"Have to" may be experienced by the receiver as dictatorial, bossy or arrogant. It may be true that the individual must complete the required forms, however, you can turn this message around by saying, "We need/I need you to complete the required forms." It's more communicative and positive to share what *you* need to proceed on their behalf, rather than what *they* must do. This approach subtly lets the receiver know that you're making an effort to be of service.

Negative Sentence #3:
"Have I got you at a bad time?"

This is one of my all time favourites. It seems positive on its face. After all, you're asking permission to proceed; you're not just jumping in without knowing if it's OK to do so. Remember to focus on what you want, and use language to reflect it. You may not get what you want each time out but this strategy will help increase the odds. "Have I got you at a bad time?" is negative because the word "bad" is used. When you call a client or colleague because you need their help, do you hope it is a *bad* time to connect? Of course not...you're hoping it's a *good* time! Then say so. Articulate this enquiry that way. "Is this a *good* time?" Magic!

Much research proves that the brain thinks in pictures and images and language brings them to life. Written language relies on letters and words (which are symbols for the pictures, ideas or concepts being described or discussed) to verbalize concepts. For example, as I sit here writing these sentences, there's a nasty, blustery and quintessentially cold Canadian winter day whirling around the two sets of windows of my corner office. Right now is a terrific time to think of Hawaii! Close your eyes right now and think of "Hawaii". What do you think of? What comes to mind? When I ask my audiences this question responses vary from grass skirts, to sun and surf, to ukuleles, to sipping long, cool drinks under thatched-roofed cabanas, and, of course, beautiful beaches that go on forever. No one has ever said that, when asked to think of "Hawaii", they thought of the letters "H", "A" "W" "A" "I" "I"! No one thinks of the symbols (the letters or word that identifies "Hawaii"); instead, they thought of the idea or concept...the picture behind the word.

Same meat, different gravy. — Beryl Miseldine Spencer

How many times have you heard someone in your workplace say something like, "Don't forget our big, important, heavy duty meeting this Monday?", or, "Don't forget to bring some goodies for Friday Treat Day?" See how even I have subtly made a negative and positive distinction between what happens on Mondays and what happens on Fridays? I unconsciously used *Monday* as an example for the heaviness of meetings, while I assigned *Friday* as an example for the lightness of treats at work! Even though I've caught myself, I've left these examples as they are to demonstrate that watching your positive word focus is a life long study; and, even if you do commit to using more and more positively focused language, you can still expect to make a few "mistakes" all along the way. But I digress. Take a look at your own "forgetful" language. Do you realize how often you choose this word to get your message across? "Forget" is the same as "bad". My mother would have said, "Same meat, different gravy". When you use the word "forget" you unintentionally bring attention to the action of "forgetting". The other person may have had no intention of forgetting, for example, the Monday meeting or Friday treats, but *now* you've gone and done it...you've suggested "forgetting" and all the subliminal imagery that goes along with it! What is it that you want them to do? *Remember!* "Remember...our big, important meeting this Monday", or "Remember to bring some goodies for Treats Day this Friday". Whether it's "bad" or "good", or "forget" versus "remember", it's always more communicative, more influential, more persuasive and inspiring to use *positively* focused words, which subconsciously trigger positive images in the minds of the people receiving your articulated messages.

Negative Sentence #4:
"You've called the wrong department. You should have called Human Resources."

Do you see the two negative focuses in this sentence? "Wrong" and "should have" are the nasty culprits here. Why do we feel the conscious or unconscious need to tell people that they are *wrong* rather than merely pointing the way ahead? The speaker goes on to say "wrong" again (with different words) when stating, "You should have," which is judgmental and may even be interpreted by the listener as haughty, condescending, arrogant or self-righteous. Is *this* what you want to put across to your colleague or client? No?

Here's the simple and positive way to put the same message across: "The correct department for your enquiry is..." As well as changing "wrong" to "correct" you've economized on words spoken.

Negative Sentence #5:
"You've completely missed my point! or, You've completely misunderstood me!"

How many times have we all heard such words loudly and aggressively expressed in meetings? How many times have you used this kind of sentence yourself? How many times have you been on the receiving end of such a declaration? Consider this scenario: You make a valuable point or suggestion in a team meeting. A team member (who, at the best of times, rubs you the wrong way) jumps on your suggestion and goes off on a tirade about why your idea couldn't work. You defend your suggestion using classic confrontational and defensive language, saying, perhaps with a little bit of attitude thrown in for good measure, that they've misunderstood you, or missed your point. There it is!

Is there a chance your teammate feels attacked? In a case like this, the listener may well feel that you're subtly saying that they're too dense to comprehend your idea. It becomes a perceived insult and triggers a dynamic that may easily become argumentative, defensive and unproductive and last long after the moment of confrontation.

Demonstrate your professionalism by carrying the banner of personal excellence in verbal communications, and use alternative language to let another know that they've missed your point. Take personal responsibility for putting across your ideas in a way others will comprehend, rather than blaming *them* for not having enough intelligence to understand *you*.

When it comes to communicating a complex, emotional or value-driven idea, it's important to realize the value of being able to articulate your idea at least two or three different ways. It may take two or three (or even four) tries before the other comes around. Here's a positive alternative to, "You've totally missed my point": "I need to put that another way", or, "Let me put it another way", or "I need to clarify my point". The bottom line is this ... work, at least from the beginning, with this philosophy: "If the receiver of my message doesn't "get it", *I* haven't communicated it well", or, to put that positively, "I need to be clearer". Yes, sometimes, there will be cases when, no matter how hard you try, someone just doesn't get the idea at all. At least start with the premise that the onus is on *you* to try, try again to communicate using words that continue to subtly honour the other.

Negative Sentence #6:
"Thank you for holding (or waiting)."

This is another of my favourites, and one in which you may see no wrong. The negative here is, "holding" or "waiting". Do *you* like to hold or wait for anything? We live in such an instant world that even waiting for two minutes seems like a minute and a half too long! I know several people who, although they don't care to confess this, will hang up and call again, feigning they were cut off, rather than hold for a couple of minutes. Are you ever required to put a colleague or client on hold while gathering information? If so, it helps to let the individual know how many minutes you expect you'll be (and, perhaps better still, offer the option of calling back once you have the requested information). But, if the caller does wish to hold, use positive words of thanks upon your return. What does that sound like? Like this: "Thanks for your *patience.*" This becomes increasingly important if you're returning to the phone to offer information to a caller who was hostile or aggressive from the start, or if you're returning to the phone with information which the caller may interpret as bad news.

Instead of expressing thanks for holding/waiting, express thanks for the caller's *patience.* Remember to always use words that create a subtle image of the behaviour and attitude you're hoping they will display. Sometimes, while the caller is on hold, they have the time to start fuming and fretting. Unaware, you return to the phone to receive a blast. It's not personal, but you're the representative of your organization in that moment, and you're the one who catches the emotional upchuck. If, at the moment of your return to the phone, you *thank* the caller for their *patience,* instead, you may just be lucky enough to assuage their fury and cause the potentially irate caller to bite his or her tongue, stay civil and listen up.

> *Words have the power to destroy or heal. When words are both true and kind, they can change our world.*
> — Buddha

Word choice can make all the difference in the response of others. Every now and then, no matter what words you use, one or two irritated callers may boom, "WELL I WASN'T PATIENT!" Not all the strategies work with all the people, all the time. Still, if using this positive alternative causes you to have a more pleasant and serene exchange with at least some of your irritable callers, it's worth the effort. Most of us know that even one agitating exchange during a workday can rattle your performance for the entire day. It might even effect how you experience your evening or off hours. Practicing, on purpose, saying, "Thank you for your patience," may just be the low cost, low effort, magical adjustment in your daily words choices that keeps you that much happier and saner during (and after) any business day. And *that* will help sustain your passion for your profession, for sure!

Negative Sentence #7:
"I think you do a great job but..."; **"I really like your ideas for this pilot project but...";** **"I see your point but...";** **"Darling I love you but...".**

What do you suppose comes next? Good news? Hardly! Yet so many of us, both personally and professionally, use "but" language, on a regular basis. The "but" word negates the first part of such sentences. In most cases, despite the fact that many people love to hide behind the, "We're all adults, here; everyone can stand constructive criticism," philosophy, many people are only twelve years old when it comes to constructive criticism (even if they won't admit it). Many of us remain a little fragile when it comes to criticism. We may learn to mask our emotions but it hits us in the gut all the same. When a colleague or a person to whom you report approaches you, saying, "Can I give you a little constructive criticism?" there's only one appropriate response...and it isn't "No, I'm too sensitive"! So we end up saying, "Yes" because it's the grown up thing to say, all the while dreading what's to follow.

Let's take a look at the very words, "constructive criticism", before even tackling the positive repackaging of such a sentence. Getting back to the idea of words creating images in the mind of the receiver of your message...use the word "criticism" and the other will wince—it's almost guaranteed. Alternatively, say "feedback", which is more neutral. It allows listeners to decide for themselves (without a feeling that you're judging) if your comments are worthy of their consideration.

Instead of bridging a two-pronged sentence with the "but" word, try one of these two strategies:

1. Build a new bridge—in other words, instead of *but*tressing your sentences, use *"a-n-d"*. For example, "I think you're doing great work *AND* I have a couple of suggestions for developing your skills even further." Changing *but* to *and* allows both expressed thoughts to be accepted and valued by the receiver.

2. If *"and"* doesn't feel right to you, try placing a period after your first shared thought. Pause, and then proceed with your second statement, eliminating *but* or *and* altogether. For example, "You're doing terrific work. (pause). Here are two suggestions for improving your results..."

You may hear people who are at odds with one another, say, "I hear you but..." followed by a long line-up of words which prove that they seemingly didn't "hear" anything the other really said, and were merely using this language as an insincere lead-in to their own, opposing viewpoint.

A champion of thoughtful communication will use an alternative strategy to put across the "but" message, without ever using the "b" word at all. The enlightened communicator uses a three-step strategy for putting across *but*less sentences.

It's all about disagreeing diplomatically:

Step 1. Paraphrase the other's position or opinion first. This means that before you state *your* opinion, you acknowledge the other's position. For example, say the following to the other: "*You* want to change our policy on this matter because..." Make the balance of this sentence a paraphrasing of what you've just heard the other say. You don't need to agree with this perspective— merely echo back to the other what you thought you heard expressed. Author, Stephen Covey (*The Seven Habits of Highly Effective People*) identifies this concept as his Habit Number Five: Seek first to understand, then to be understood.

Step 2. Demonstrate that you value their contribution and thoughts even though yours differ. Use words that specifically express that, even though you feel differently, you understand their perspective. Be specific and detailed in your expression of what you appreciate about the other's perspective: "I see your point about changing our policy on...because we need to..."

The completion of this detailed sentence positively supports at least some aspect of what the other is saying. Such a lead-in to your own position tells the listener that you've taken their perspective into account.

Step 3. State your position or opinion next. Do this seamlessly by pausing between steps two and three. Example: "I see your point about changing our policy because I know we will need to..." Step three response would follow: "I feel", "my opinion focuses on...", "I think...", or "I want..." This is a bit tricky because most people automatically use the "but" word as a bridge between steps two and three. Remember, as well, that the *but* word has a lot of relatives. "However", "although", and "never-the-less" are all first cousins of *but!* Can you think of any second cousins?

Here's a summary of the three-sentence formula for expressing your thoughts of disagreement with diplomacy:

1. "You feel..." (think, want, etc.) tells the listener, "I'm listening to your opinion and I take it into account."
2. "I understand that..." (or "I can see why you feel that way."), says, "I hear you and respect your opinion."
At this point you must continue with details of *why* you understand the other's perspective. Once this sentence is complete, take a "*but*less" pause.
3. "I feel" (think, want) says, "I don't agree, but I value you, so let's continue to talk and exchange ideas in a respectful and receptive manner.

This strategy works well whenever you find yourself at the delicate crossroads of differing opinions with an individual you generally respect. These three sentences will not fix all the differences between you and another, but these sentences *will* help keep hearts and minds open to more communication. Did you notice I used the *but* word in the preceding sentence? I did so, and point this out to you now, to illustrate that there *are* times when you'll wish to purposefully negate the first part of your sentence to specifically highlight the second.

Negative Sentence #8:
"I'm either away from my desk or on my phone, so please leave a message and I'll try to get back to you as soon as possible."

This is one of my favourite pet peeves. What does, "I'll *try* to get back to you as soon as possible," mean, anyway? There's a classic challenge many workshop leaders use. A participant is asked to "try" to pick up a pen. Befuddled, the participant picks it up, all the while wondering, "What's the catch?" The facilitator says, "No...don't *actually* pick up the pen...just show me *trying* to pick it up!". Ahhh! "Trying" is a non-action, a vague illusion. There's only picking it up or not. There's only calling back or not—no *trying*. You either do or you don't keep your recorded promise. And the proof is in your action.

Now let's take a look at the second part of this classic recorded greeting..."as soon as possible". This is easy to say, and is almost a standard expression; it doesn't tell the caller anything about when to expect a response. "As soon as possible" could mean later that day or later that year! Many organizations now insist that employees record outgoing messages that promise a return call within 24 hours. To this, many an employee may snicker behind a covered hand, feeling that it's hardly likely that they'll keep this promise either. And yes, many a cynical receiver of the promised "24 hour returned call" may think, "I'll believe *that* when I hear it." Perhaps the call isn't always returned in the promised 24-hour timeframe, however, at least this level of articulated commitment is a step in the right direction (and may cause you to work harder at returning calls within the promised time).

Under promise and over deliver. — Anonymous

Positively alter this sentence by increasing your integrity about keeping your recorded promise. *Under promise and over deliver.* Instead of saying, "I'm away from my desk," say, "I must be close by and I want to return your call." If you're not close by—if you're in a two-hour meeting—rather than saying, "I'm out of the office at a meeting this morning," say, "I'm in a meeting this morning. I'll be back in the office this afternoon and will return your call then." You could also choose to eliminate the "out of the office" part, altogether, and just record the part about when you *will* be available. Most people don't really want to know where you are, they just want to know when you'll be back and return their call! Give them some hope (and some concrete parameters) about when that will be.

Negative Sentence #9:
"I'm sorry it's taken me so long to get back to you but I've been so busy, and it's been so crazy around here, and I was on vacation, too!"

Most everyone I know can confess to using this line (or some variation thereof). Wouldn't it be bizarrely refreshing for a person to say, "I know that it's taken me two months to return your call. Quite frankly, it was just not important enough for me to return it until now!" Ouch. That sounds so mean, and unkind—but refreshingly honest, too. The reality is, we do return the calls we want to return, or feel we must, busy or not. Hiding behind, "It's been crazy around here," may be the truth but, to the receiver, it's meaningless. Forego the knee-jerk desire to defend your tardiness with that cliché, and say, "I'm finally returning your call!" The caller will already assume you've been busy—after all, you've taken this long to return their call, haven't you? They're probably delighted to have you on the line *now*, so focus on that in your words, instead.

Negative Sentence #10:
"If you have any questions, don't hesitate to call."

The negative message in this instance is "don't hesitate." It creates an image of hesitation. Many people may feel obliged to express this sentiment but secretly hope that the person won't call. If you champion the idea of using inviting, positive language and/or if you really *do* need the person to call if they have questions, say, "If you have any questions, *please feel free* to call me."

Remember to always ask for what you do want rather than draw attention to what you don't. Use the word "free" on purpose. "Free" is a concept that everybody loves—just look at the people lining up for free nibblies at the grocery store's promotional kiosks any given weekend. There they are...all kinds of people lining up for food that doesn't really appeal to them, merely because it's free! I rest my case. Need more convincing about the power of "free"? Just ask a sales professional; "free" is one of the 14 most influential and persuasive words used to get to "yes" and close a deal.

Learning how to turn autopilot, negative sentences into consciously chosen positive ones will help inspire and influence more open and pleasant communications between you and others. If you become a student of this strategy for life, your communications with others will stay that much more harmonious, and *that* will automatically make way for you to feel more joy about your daily work!

Always do your best. What you plant now you will harvest later. — Og Magdino

2

Passion Point #2:
Project Professional Self-Worth

As is our confidence, so is our capacity.
— William Hazlitt

Some people have quite an inflated opinion of their professional worth. I'm reminded of one of my favourite comics, which metaphorically illustrates this point so nicely. Imagine an "out-of-shape/pear-shaped dude", stripped down to his zany boxer shorts, sunken chest, protruding abdomen (with just a hint of belly button gaping out from under his too small tee-shirt), with leg stubble, to boot. He's flashing a big toothy grin as he flexes his muscles in front of his full-length mirror. To his delight (but, one imagines, not to his surprise) the image he sees reflected back at him is one of a man with an Arnold Schwartzenegger physique! Some things just aren't what they seem.

Some people in the workplace believe they make tremendously valuable contributions to their team and organization, but as in the image just described, they're only "legends in their own minds".

I believe, however, that most employees' truth is captured *not* through this "out-of-shape dude" comic image, but rather by the following Gary Larson comic visual: an ancient, scowling faced Macedonian woman sits at a table, half-eaten drumstick in hand, scolding her grown-up son. She's yelling, "And another thing...I want you to be more assertive! I'm tired of everyone calling you Alexander the *Pretty Good!*" He's not supposed to be Alexander the "pretty good" he's supposed to be Alexander the *Great!*

It's likely that your contribution in the workplace isn't just "pretty good", it's probably great! The trouble is, many people feel that it's arrogant to trumpet their own contribution—it's alright if another does it for you, but not to do it for yourself. In fact, most of us easily sing another's praises but not our own. Now is the time to admit the truth about what you bring to the professional table. Your organization needs you, now more than ever, to identify and acknowledge your professional qualities, knowledge, skills and abilities. No more hiding your professional light under a bushel! It's not conceit—it's good for your soul and for your organization, too! Employers desperately need employees who clearly understand their professional contribution; this awareness not only elevates the individual's sense of empowerment, it also acts as a guidepost for others to do the same. Empowered employees help organizations move efficiently and effectively towards their goals.

> *Use what talents you possess; the woods would be very silent if no birds sang there except those that sang best.* — Henry Van Dyke

How easy is it for you (and/or your staff) to answer the following questions? These questions will help employees develop instant awareness of the fine contribution they make.

Answer these questions for yourself, and also consider facilitating a team session around these same questions, where each member would first write down their answers privately and then—to up the ante— read their written words aloud to their teammates:

1. What professional abilities and gifts come to me easily?
2. What professional skills do I demonstrate better than most people?
3. How have I grown professionally over the past year (and don't say, "I've grown *out!*"; there are often one or two sassy people in my audiences who love to respond this way)?
4. What's the most important professional lesson I've learned

this year, so far, and how am I applying it now, or intend to apply this wisdom in the year to come?

5. What are the most difficult things I've accomplished in my current position?
6. Of what workplace accomplishment am I most proud?
7. When it comes to my professional contribution, about what would I most like to receive compliments?

Encouraging and facilitating sessions in which staff members complete these questions, and then tell each other their answers, reminds staff of their important contributions and may help them through challenging times. At the very most, such an exercise may make a measurable difference in an employee's day-to-day performance. At the very least, when a staff member may be feeling blue and unappreciated, rereading his or her answers to these questions may be just the medicine for regaining pride in his/her contribution, no matter what storm front is moving though the local workplace community.

What you think of yourself is much more important than what others think of you. — Seneca

Your job and your professional contribution, no matter how "high up" or frontline your position, are important to your employer's success. If they weren't—especially in these days of economic uncertainty and budget consciousness—you'd already be gone. Remember *that* the next time you're unsure of how your contribution fits into the organization's big picture. It may also help to keep these eloquent and inspired words close by:

"If a man is a street sweeper, he should sweep the streets even as Michelangelo painted, or Beethoven composed music, or Shakespeare wrote poetry.

He should sweep streets so well that all the hosts of heaven and earth will pause to say, here lived a great street sweeper who did his job well."
— Martin Luther King Jr.

Keep on "sweeping"!

Think "Me Inc." Think!

One idea that's been around for a long time (but keeps getting rediscovered) is the self-managed career; 'You've got to look after your own career prospects; nobody else is going to.' Today that idea is being taken a step further. You had better not only be taking care of your own future, but also looking at yourself as if you were self-employed. — William Bridges, *JobShift: How to Prosper in a Workplace Without Jobs*

Think "Me Inc." think—it sounds like something Dr. Seuss might have suggested! Pretend you're self-employed, even if you never intend to hang out your independent professional shingle. Amazing things will happen to your attitude and behaviour if you think of yourself in this way. Pretend that your client (a.k.a. your actual employer) has provided you such a grand contract that you don't have time to take on additional business.

I remember when I first came across this suggestion. I was working in Organizational Development/Training and Development within an organization of 5500 employees. The concept provided an immediate awakening about how I could think and act at work. From that point on, although I continued in that position for a few more years, I'd already mentally quit my job and joined the ranks of the self-employed. Did I rip-off my employer because of this shift in thinking? Did my employer or my workshop participants, get less service after I started "Me Inc?" On the contrary! When I quietly declared myself, "Me/Nina Spencer Inc.", I began seeing workshop participants as my clients and primary consumers of my professional services, in a whole new and enlightened way. I felt professionally reborn and rededicated to doing my best possible work. It was as though I was experiencing the exhilaration of a brand new job.

Thinking "Me. Inc." think will elevate your status in your own mind's eye to that of *partner* with your employer. Your new status as organizational *partner* can make you that much more interested in your organization's goals, objectives, mission and values. *Make* yourself think this way. It may make the difference between 99% commitment to your work and 100% commitment. Once, many years ago, a very wise man told me that 100% commitment to anything is a cinch, but 99% commitment is a _ _ _ _ _! Ain't it the truth? Have you ever been 99% committed to something or someone? At least, on occasion, hasn't that *one* percent of doubt wielded amazing power and influence to contaminate the other 99%? Total commitment to, "Me Inc.", thinking may make the difference between going home at the end of the day exhausted and deflated, or going home joyful and fulfilled. Thinking "Me Inc." think will empower you to become aware of your ability to effect change and rekindle passion for your profession.

By the time I actually became *Nina Spencer & Associates, Conference Keynotes and Workshops*, my mental and literal leap from employee to businessperson was minimal. I'm not suggesting you should consider "Me. Inc" think as a weigh-station to quitting your job, but I *am* suggesting that it will go far in improving your day-in and day-out sense of professional autonomy, maturity and gratification. Even if you're someone else's employee all the rest of your working days...*you really have always worked for yourself!* Now, start believing and demonstrating it. You, your employer, fellow employees, internal and external clients will benefit from this shift in your outlook.

> *Think enthusiastically about everything, but especially about your job. If you do, you'll put a touch of glory in your life. If you love your job with enthusiasm you'll shake it to pieces. You'll love it into greatness. You'll upgrade it. You'll fill it with prestige and power.*
> — Norman Vincent Peale

Further Exploring Your Professional Self-Worth by Way of The Johari Window Model

> *It is never too late to be what you might have become.*
> — George Eliot

When it comes to understanding your professional self-worth, it helps to know yourself a little more each day. It also helps if you let others in your circle of interaction and influence get to know *you*. Playing your workplace cards chronically close to your chest, maintaining a poker face and subscribing to a siege mentality may be dangerous to your workplace satisfaction and success. It may even undo all you've worked to build.

Why do some people insist on going it alone at all times and at all costs? Why do some people feel that maintaining a "professional" demeanor with colleagues, clients and customers means being *technically* polite and gracious but really being cool, distant and veiled? Why is it that some workplace colleagues are convinced that self-disclosure and the sharing of some free information about themselves is the *worst* thing they could possibly do? These are definitely politically correct and fragile times, and there are definitely times when it's smart to keep your thoughts and feeling to yourself; however, I suggest there are more benefits than pitfalls to building workplace relationships and letting people in.

George Radwanski, until the spring of 2003, was Canada's Privacy Commissioner. Released from his duties in June of that year amidst allegations of expense account gouging (extravagant lunches and numerous trips) and because of public outrage over his non-payment of over one half million dollars in taxes, Radwanski insisted that he was a victim of "character assassination" and "vicious, untrue and distorted" allegations. He went on to say, "The failure of anyone in a position of authority in Parliament, government or the public service to speak out or intervene in my defense...has made it impossible for me to do my job." Canada's *Globe and Mail* newspaper columnist, John Ibbitson, recounted Radwanski's complaints in his June 24, 2003 column, *Commissioner lacked friends in both high and low places*. Ibbitson retorted, "But that, Mr. Radwanski, is exactly the point. You made everyone mad at you, and when you got into trouble you expected them to rush to your aid. Don't you know anything about office politics?" I guess he didn't. Even his own staff circulated a petition to oust him!

On the flip side, at about the very same time Mr. Radwanski was ushered out the door, a popular Toronto-based morning radio personality named Erin Davis was also fired. Toronto Star's Entertainment reporter Nick McCabe-Lokos, (in a July 9, 2003 article) reported she was called at her summer cottage on a Saturday and told not to come into work on Monday—just like that! What followed, wrote McCabe-Lokos, was the delivery of more than 3000 fan emails and over 90 pages of complaints on her employer's web site message board, which was later temporarily taken down. Although loyal listeners may not have been able to return this local radio celebrity to her position, it must have been comforting for Ms. Davis to know that so many people cared to protest and boycott the station.

When it comes to the importance of the "likeability factor", consider the amazing "P. S." to this "Erin Davis" story: two years later (in the summer of 2005) the extraordinary happened. After 24 months of sliding morning ratings at the radio station in question, and after 24 months of sustained loyal listener complaints and insistence that the station had made a big mistake, the station's General Manager and Program Director, Julie Adam, released the following words on both the station's website and in a general media release: "Have you ever made a mistake at work? Well, about 2 years ago, I made a mistake. A big one. In June, 2003, I fired Erin Davis. When the decision was made, we thought it was the right thing to do. We believed that the station needed to be rejuvenated and that it should start with the Morning Show. Over time, we found out that it just wasn't possible to replace Erin Davis. The bond between Erin and CHFI was simply too strong, and we were wrong to underestimate the power of her relationship with the audience." Apparently the odds of this kind of retraction and reinstatement in radio are "slim to none". Always remember the potential power and influence of your likeability factor. I suspect Ms. Davis will attest to that!

People are most likely to rally around if you're likeable. Sharing appropriate, tasteful and well-timed personal information in the workplace, builds trust, relationship and loyalty—traits most individuals and organizations say they champion.

To what extent do *you* share personal information in the workplace? To what extent are you comfortable with appropriate and tasteful self-disclosure? Do you see the value of at least *some* information sharing and self-disclosure in building more collaborative workplace relationships?

The Johari Awareness Model or Johari Window (derived from the names of the psychologists, Joseph Luft and Harry

Ingham, who created it) is a classic framework for gaining insight about how we relate to others in the workplace and elsewhere, and discovering more about ourselves that we didn't realize was there, all along.

> *Life is like a 10 speed bike. We all have gears we never use.* — Charles Schultz

To understand how this model applies to your workplace relationships, imagine yourself as a square, leaded window with four distinct panes of glass. It's through this window that you look out onto the world, and through which others look in on you. When you communicate with colleagues or customers, the quality of the interaction depends on what you reveal through your windowpanes.

The model implies that each quadrant/each pane of glass, is equal in size. Unknowingly, however, you may be setting up your personal window in such a way that the panes of glass are irregular or disproportioned. The good news is that you *can* learn to adjust the balance of your windowpanes.

The Public Arena: The real me/You know these things and I know these things

> *What I want for my life now is for it to be simple, without secrets. I want to be who I really am, with everyone, all the time.* — E. L. Doctorow

Ingham and Luft labelled the upper left quadrant of their Johari Window Model, the *Public Arena*. It's in this quadrant that we *consciously* reveal ourselves to others. It's in the Public Arena where we're most charismatic, most magnetic and most "attractive" to others, either personally or professionally. When we're looking onto the world from the Public Arena, we appear (and truly *are*) most comfortable and confident in our own skin...and it shows!

A play on two sentences is applied to each of the quadrants. For the Public Arena the two sentences are, "*I know these things* about me", and, "*You* know *these things* about me". If only we all operated from the Public Arena all of the time! Would it be a good thing or a bad one—I wonder? We could end up like Jim Carey's character in the movie *Liar, Liar.* For a full day, he was under a magic spell and could not tell a lie—at work or anywhere else. You can imagine what happened!

So, yes, there are times when you know *how* to operate from the Public Arena, but, being the politically savvy individual that you are, choose not to. You keep your thoughts and feelings to yourself, or tow the company line, because it's expedient to do so.

The question is, to what extent are the current dimensions of your Public Arena windowpane helping or hindering your team, customers, clients or your personal day-to-day workplace satisfaction? Could broadening your Public Arena windowpane improve your satisfaction and results?

The Mask: The who I pretend to be/I know these things about me, but you don't

> *Masquerade, painted faces on parade, masquerade,*
> *hide your face so the world will never find you.*
> — From the song "Masquerade"/Andrew Llloyd
> Webber's Phantom of the Opera

Most of us feel more comfortable with some colleagues and/or clients than others. With these people we're more inclined to operate from our Public Arena windowpane. With *others*, people tend to shrink their Public Arena windowpane and operate from the lower left windowpane called Mask. *I* call this quadrant, "Who I Pretend to Be." In this windowpane, you keep your cards close to your chest, *masking* your true self.

The play on sentences for Mask are, "I know these things about me", but "*You* don't know these things about me". There is definitely a time and place when it's wise to mask your attitude and preferred behaviour. However, are you truly aware of the extent to which you do this? Is the degree to which you mask justified or merely habitual (perhaps based on your upbringing or past workplace experiences)? Does the degree to which you mask help or hinder the results you want for yourself, your team, clients/customers and employer's overall success? What positive results might occur if you let down your mask a little more?

The Blind Spot: You know these things but I don't

Always listen to a man when he describes the faults of others. Often times, most times, without realization, he's describing his own, revealing himself.
— Malcolm Forbes

The upper right quadrant of the Johari Window is entitled, *Blind* or, as I like to say, *Blind Spot*. Everyone has blind spots. What would happen if you decided that you were fed up with checking your mirrors while changing lanes on busy highways? You'd get hit—right? It's the same with your metaphoric Blind Spots. The truth is—although you may not like it—*everyone else* gets to see you in a way that you will *never* see yourself. That's because you're on the inside of the window, looking out and they're on the outside looking in! When it comes to knowing ourselves, much of the time we're too close to the material.

The two sentences at play for Blind are, "You know these things about me" but "I don't know these things about me!" Some may argue, "But I *can* see what others see by videotaping myself at a team meeting or during a presentation!" N'uh-uh...these examples only give you a watered down, two-dimensional version of what others all get to see, and it's not in real time. Sometimes others can see things about our attitudes, behaviours and performance that we'll never be able to see for ourselves. This is exactly why 360 degree feedback models have become so popular. It's also why progressive organizations care to conduct customer satisfaction surveys and take action on the results.

Facilitative questions for examining your own blind spots could include, "Do I accept that I probably have some blind spots about my attitudes and behaviours which may be standing in the way of my desired results, or the impression I wish to make upon others? Who can I ask/who do I trust or respect to share their observations about my performance so that I can make desired adjustments? What positive results could occur for me if I discovered *and acted* on more of my blind spots?"

If we all did what we were capable of doing we would literally astonish ourselves. — Thomas Edison

The Unknown: My hidden potential/You don't know these things about me and neither do I (yet)

There is a great deal of unmapped country within us. — George Eliot

The lower-right quadrant is *Unknown*. I like to call it, *Hidden Potential*. The play on sentences here? "*I* don't know these things about me", and, "*You* don't know these things about me, either". That's why it's the "unknown"! But I like to add an extra word to these two sentences..."*Yet!*"

Where is it written that what is currently unknown to you about your knowledge, skills, abilities, talents, capabilities, gifts, strengths, etc., has to stay that way your whole life long? What positive results would occur for yourself, your team, organization, etc., if you discovered your hidden potential?"

Remember, the model is presented—for argument's sake— as though you spend 25% of your work life/private life in each of the four quadrants. It really doesn't need to be that way. In which of the four quadrants would you experience the greatest amount of comfort, confidence and professional satisfaction? From which quadrant would you most likely make a powerful and real contribution? The Public Arena. And so it's your Public Arena quadrant you want to expand. Think of someone you admire who, in your opinion, makes a powerful positive difference. From which window do *they* operate? One person that often comes to mind, for me, is Oprah Winfrey. She lays it all on the line, candid as the day is long. The gossip rags never seem to get much on Oprah because she tells all about herself! Whether you're a fan or not, you must acknowledge that she has tremendous charisma and a high likeability factor for millions. Oprah is a quintessential example of an individual who operates largely out of her Public Arena windowpane.

> *The self-explorer, whether he wants to or not, becomes the explorer of everything else. He learns to see himself, but suddenly, provided he was honest, all the rest appears, and it is rich as he was, and, as a final crowning, richer.* — Elias Canetti

Who operates that way in *your* life? Who do you know and admire whose Public Arena window represents 50% or more of their entire window? How big is *your* Public Arena window? Would you like to expand it? Here's how:

1. Give yourself permission to push down on the horizontal edge of your Public Arena pane, expanding the space for your real self to shine through, and shrinking your Mask. Do this by deciding, today, with whom, where and when, you will deliver a little more *real you* and a little less *mask*, when next you meet.

2. Expand the right/eastern border of your Public Arena windowpane by shrinking your Blind Spot; by considering and opening up to feedback from others with whom you interact.

3. Look at what happens next....if you push down on your Mask and shrink your Blind Spot, you'll *automatically* increase the square footage of your Public Arena; as a spin-off effect, you'll automatically tap into and become aware of some of your personal Unknown.

Reducing your Mask and Blind Spot automatically increases your Public Arena and, residually, decreases your personal Unknown, allowing more of your hidden potential to shine through. Hypothetically (and, in reality, if you *really* want to work on it all the rest of your days) your "Public Arena" pane can be as much as two thirds or more of your total personal "window". You're the one who gets to decide.

The more you tastefully and appropriately share with others, the stronger the relationship that is built. You may be more likely to honk your horn and wave your fist in anger at that seemingly incompetent driver in front of you if that individual is a stranger, than you would if he or she were your friend. Why the difference? Relationship.

It's especially when you experience one of the crises that life throws your way, that you realize the value of building warm and sincere personal and professional relationships. And everyone could use a little help and support from some*one* who cares when crises occur. It's not *why* one should do this...but it certainly is a fine benefit. It's the old Stephen Covey metaphor of the, "Emotional Bank Account". You put your deposits in along the way—and watch the compound interest grow—so that there's something from which to draw upon when you need it. And, sooner or later, you'll probably need it!

It takes courage to grow up and turn out who you really are. — e. e. cummings

3

Passion Point #3:
Protect Your Sense of Humour

> *Laughter and good humour are the canaries in the mine of commerce. If you, your employees, customers and vendors don't have a good time, if the laughter has died, you're in the wrong business.*
> — Tips from A Maverick Entrepreneur

When was the last time you had a good belly laugh with colleagues? Is it hard to remember? The gut-splitting group laugh can help whole teams through difficult times. Days, weeks, months or even years later, the mere mention of the funny trigger word, action or event can transport all those who shared in the original laughter back in time. When it comes to team spirit and team bonding, most *anything* that brings the team closer together is a good thing.

The old school of thought espoused that if you were laughing and goofing around at work, then productivity was suffering, but a magical transformation really does occur when people lighten up and laugh together. That's one of the primary reasons why regular team meetings and branch or divisional professional development days are a good idea. This is also why good professional speakers spend time carefully choosing the right "opener", and the right blend of humour and content in their presentations—they want to make 'em laugh and help the team bonding experience stick!

You don't need to teach people to be funny. You only have to give them permission. — Dr. Harvey Mindess

Why not consciously champion and contribute to humour in your workplace? It'll help you feel a little momentary passion for your profession, and it'll help your team elevate its commitment to one another, and to your branch's or division's purpose and cause. Why not create opportunities for humour with staff *who do not work together* but who work for the same organization, too. You may help break down walls and increase interdivisional or interregional communication and co-operation.

Up until age 40 you control the lines on your face. After 40, the lines on your face control you!
— Abraham Lincoln

Now, if you're over forty, don't fret (it'll only make you more wrinkly), because the message from Lincoln's quote is symbolic rather than literal. Up until a certain point in your life, you can turn your thinking and attitudes and behaviours around; but there *will* come a day when you've practiced so hard and for so long at frowning and scrunching up your face that you won't be able to straighten it out without a quarterly Botox injection! "If you keep on pulling those faces your face is going to stay that way!", so many mothers through the years have scolded their children. And that's exactly what Lincoln was suggesting. Give conscious consideration to the daily faces you pull.

Wrinkles should merely indicate where smiles have been. — Mark Twain

And, by the way, Coco Chanel said, "Nothing great happens until after you're forty", so, do take heart, whether you're this side or that side of forty!

The Less You Laugh, The Less You Laugh

Life is too serious to be taken seriously. — Oscar Wilde

Do you complain about laughing too much at work? Do you ever go home at the end of a particularly jovial day and say, "That's it! I'm not going in to work tomorrow because I laughed too hard at work today, and I need a rest to protect myself from that sort of workplace energy?" I bet not.

Demonstrate your sense of humour to yourself and others. Humour is as good for your health as it is for your spirit. "Three to five minutes of laughter doubles your heart rate—equal to three minutes on a rowing machine," notes Dr. William Fry. What would *you* rather do? I've heard on occasion that as much as 80% of all physically diagnosed illness has a stress component—and when you're stressed you're *not* laughing.

Most of us understand and appreciate the value of physical fitness and a healthy diet (and it's important to exercise and eat right to be as healthy as possible), but you can help yourself get and stay in shape with a daily dose of laughter as well. Perhaps (Snow White and) The Seven Dwarfs' song, *Whistle While You Work*, says it all!

When I was 41 I was diagnosed with cancer. That was the bad news. The good news (thanks to early detection by way of an annual physical check-up) was that it was very treatable, isolated to one area and was caught early enough. It was a scare and whack on the side of the head for me just the same.

Before I was diagnosed, and in typical fashion of most 30-somethings, I worked hard and was constantly juggling different parts of my life; I lived frenetically busy days. So what— doesn't everyone? Don't most of us (or at least many of us) go to bed too late, get up too early, skip a meal here or there and pray to God that we remember to be where we're supposed to be and when we're supposed to be there? Can *you* relate? With such frenetic daily pace and constant agenda, one is also supposed to remember to *laugh* everyday? Maybe I would have remembered, myself, if I'd put it in my planner! The bottom line is that I frequently short-changed myself on daily laughter in my "pre-cancer" days.

Of all the days, the day on which one has not laughed
is the one most surely wasted.
— Sabastien-Roch Nicolas de Chamfort

During my weeklong stay in hospital recovering from surgery, I met another patient, whom I'll call Gary. Gary had been there for six weeks and was destined to stay put for at least another four. Like old veterans comparing war wounds, we flashed our abdominal scars lined with surgical staples. I had 19 staples to show off but *he had 54!* This was a 40-something man at the top of his career, in the highest levels of management at a well-known and respected organization. He was charming, smart, and prosperous. He had a beautiful family with three children under 10 and a lovely stay-at-home wife who understood the demands of his profession and supported him all the way.

Typically, he left for work before the kids were up in the morning and wasn't back until they'd gone to bed. Although technically he *lived* with his family, he really just slept there, except on weekends. On the weekends, he was a model husband and father and did his best to squish in all the quality activity he could muster. Gary convinced himself to embrace the "it's not the quantity of time I dedicate to my family...it's the quality!" philosophy. And it worked...until, for unknown reasons, a large portion of the lining of his intestines started to weaken.

The first few times Gary was struck with excruciating abdominal pains, he was fortunate his office was only five minutes from a hospital, so he was saved and patched up to live another day. But the doctors warned Gary that he would die if he ever had an attack and could not reach an emergency room quickly. He was a walking time bomb. The doctors knew it, and so did Gary. He agreed to take the three months off of work to undergo reconstructive surgery.

The part of Gary's story that touched me most? He realized that it had taken a significant illness to slow down enough to remember how much he loved his wife. He told me that they'd played more games, and had more heart-to-heart talks during his six weeks in hospital, than in the previous 20 years, and he saw his kids everyday, too. He told me he was falling in love with is wife all over again. On top of all that, we both agreed that, although it hurt to laugh, being stuck in the hospital (sitting or lying around, or shuffling as slow as tortoises down the halls and back), gave us plenty of time to chuckle!

What a wonderful life I've had...I only wish I'd realized it sooner. — Colette

We spent a fair amount of time together during my stay. Sometimes we crept down the hall at such a snail's pace, taking each other and our respective I.V. poles for a walk, that we got too tired to turn back; we'd often have to stop and sit in the day room, to catch our wind and strength for the journey "home" to our rooms. It was in this "pit stop" room that we had most of our spontaneous chats and revelations about what good had come out of our illnesses.

On my seventh day without food (three days before my surgery and four days afterwards), I started whining and complaining and hallucinating about a dry slice of toast...*anything* that would give me the pleasure of chewing! I just wanted the sensation and joy of experiencing food once more. I was on the brink of passing the big test for crossing over to the world of the eating. All I had to do was report (honestly) that I had passed wind! The beginning of normalcy was mine for the taking if I could only get a sign—a fart (forgive me for this, but that's the blunt truth of it!). My *life*...for a fart! That's all I needed to do, but it was easier said than done, and I couldn't lie about such a thing just because I was seduced by the thought of a little bowl of hospital-style rubbery Jell-o or bland rice pudding! So I waited and wished and hoped and prayed and, all along the way, Gary kept asking me, "How's the old fart doing today?" We laughed lots and, although at first my family and friends found it a little embarrassing for me to talk in such a taboo way, eventually we *all* started having good belly laughs about Nina's "windy" wish! When my wish was finally answered, it was one o'clock in the morning, but, for me, it was the beginning of a whole new day...like hearing I'd won the lottery, so I just *had* to call home and report the good news regardless of the hour:

"Food tomorrow!"

Gary was so happy for me, too! Isn't it funny that if I'd met him two weeks earlier, we'd have never shared such conversation, nor would we have flashed our bare and stapled bellies at one another! Yet, despite my good fortune and the Jell-o and tea breakfast I had the following morning, poor Gary could only look on. He was at least another three weeks away from food and, at that time, a mere *muffin* could possibly kill him. Yet, we both laughed and saw the humour in it all. The laughter was good for us both, and it was good for our families and friends, too. It helped them realize that they didn't need to show up with worried, sad and sympathetic looks on their faces. Sharing in our smiles and laughter was the very best way they could help us heal.

Always laugh when you can. It is cheap medicine.
— Lord Byron

I never did see or hear from Gary after I left the hospital. That's OK. I believe that some connections are only for the duration and then they're complete. I'm sharing his story with you now, so, in a way, we're still connected. I suppose he could be dead but I think he's alive. He told me that once he was all fixed up he intended to do some serious thinking about his professional life. He said he secretly knew that he wouldn't return to the endless hours of work that his position demanded. He decided he would find a way to have his professional cake, and eat it, too—and that would mean seeing more of his family and friends, and making more time for laughter than he had in the past two decades. I think I can hear him laughing right now.

When I returned home to eight weeks of convalescence, we made plenty of time for all sorts of card games, Scrabble, Monopoly and the like. Until my surgery, these were the kinds of games we only played at the summer cottage. Why would you play such games at *home*, when you could be on the phone, watching TV, chatting on-line or surfing—right? The kitchen table, and these resurrected playful events, became a new source of daily laughter. I'm glad to say that years later, the decks of cards, Cribbage board, Monopoly, Scrabble (and

Scrabble Dictionary!), Backgammon, Chess, Battleship, Yahtzee, Scattagories, Pictionary, Scruples and Trivial Pursuit have *never* been put properly away since 1999! Our new/old example of how to get a "cheap laugh" has caught on with our friends, our neighbours and anyone else who happens to spend more than a couple of hours at our home. If you come to our house, you *will* be sucked into a game of one sort or another, I promise you...and you *will* have a terrific belly laugh. It's guaranteed! And you'll *like* it!

> *The most important decision you make is to be of good humour.* —Voltaire

Go For the Laughs

We accept that worry and stress can cause stomach ulcers. We accept that chronic temper tantrums can lead to high blood pressure and heart attack. Yet, for many, it's still a stretch to believe that our own *thinking* can contribute to illness.

"Although humour may not be a cure for cancer, there is clinical evidence that laughter can mobilize our body defenses and reduce pain...research supports that laughter is a natural tranquilizer. There is a direct correlation between laughter and levels of catecholamines in the blood, which cause the release of endorphins in our brain. Endorphines are nature's best built-in pain killer". This, according to Doctor Terry L. Paulson, author of "Making Humour Work: Take Your Job Seriously and Yourself Lightly".

The release of endorphins, through exercise or laughter, has been known to strengthen the immune system. Dr. Paulson notes that ancient Greeks, in their healing centers, included a visit to the "home of comedians" as part of their "therapeia process." Laughing *can* save your life! As Norman Cousins, a now-renowned cancer survivor (thanks to, among other things, his insistence on reading jokes and funny stories each and every day of his cancer experience), said, "Laughter interrupts the panic cycle of an illness". And anything that stops the panic is a good thing.

Laughter is a tranquilizer with no side-effects.
— Arnold H. Glasgow

What if it's not *your* lack of sense of humour that's the problem? What if you're doing fine but one or more of your colleagues are in humour trouble? Many years ago I was given a cartoon that showed two sad porcupines facing each other, lamenting, "Just once, I'd like to be petted". To me, the message was, "Just once I wish someone at work would see beyond my miserable, prickly exterior and realize that I have tender insides, just like yours." I suggest that there are probably a few *porcupines* in your workplace disguised as *people*—do you agree? You know to whom I'm referring: people so prickly that everyone avoids them at all cost. They're so chronically negative, so disagreeable and downright untouchable that they can lower the enthusiasm and spirits of an entire team.

You'd think that eight people on a team would each wield one eighth of the power and influence of that team. That's a bit of a myth. Not all team members' influence is created equal. One or two negative, humourless people on a team may wield more power to impede the team's momentum than the other six, no matter how hard the six strive to rise above.

So what are you going to do about those porcupines you encounter at work? Yes, it's true that life's circumstances may have given the porcupine good reason to be miserable, but you can let them bring you and all your teammates down or you can start asking yourself these questions:

- How can I use *my* sense of humour to reach out to this person?

- In what two ways can I demonstrate my sense of humour and draw others in, this very week?

- How can I tastefully foster or facilitate a sense of humour in my workplace that draws others out of their shells this very week?

Remember, the porcupines can bring *you* down, or you can bring *them* up. You can't wait for the other guy to make things better—it may never happen—*you* have to take the initiative.

A person without humour is like a car without shock absorbers. — Anonymous

Laughter and humour build rapport, and rapport builds compassion and commitment; and commitment, over time, builds trust. It's that simple. It's hard to dislike someone with whom you regularly laugh.

Team meetings are a natural and obvious place to work on building relationships. Take advantage of these opportunities to do more than "take care of business".

Here are four suggestions for increasing camaraderie and rapport during team meetings:

1. **Share Passages or Quotes to Create Dialogue:** Find some funny quotes and passages and put them where you'll see them to remind you how you wish to interact with others. Where appropriate, consider a "Round Robin" of humourous quotes at the beginning or end of team meetings. Confess why your contribution strikes your funny bone and is pertinent. At the very least, sharing quotes and funny stories will give you all a good, shared laugh. At the very most, these quotes may give team members a lead-in to discuss tender issues.

2. **Use Visuals to Introduce or Underscore Important Points:** Try kicking off a routine team meeting with a comic on the topic(s) of discussion (there are plenty of comics in most daily newspapers that touch on issues at the heart of business today). Remove the caption and have team members brainstorm their own, then share the original caption in your debrief. Try it in reverse, too. Have team members *draw their own* visual from a caption you provide (without any image). You can share the original image in your debrief, if you like or, perhaps don't even bother revealing the original image at all. Merely provide participants with a topical caption, and see what visuals materialize.

3. **Props Goes the Leader:** Look around your office or house for things that symbolically illustrate and strengthen key

messages you wish to address in team meetings. As a speaker and facilitator I've successfully (and hilariously at times) used full cans of pop, balloons, play phones, balls, plastic dinosaurs and other frightening and sweet "beasties" from my kids' toy box to poignantly drive home my key messages. I've even used Eastern European Babushka Dolls to make a serious point in a light-hearted way!

4. **Team Member Reveal Thy Self:** Self-disclosure helps strengthen bonds among team members. Revealing appropriate personal information makes you three dimensional and more "real" in the eyes of another. Humourous or light hearted self-disclosure helps to reveal your humanity (as discussed earlier under the "Johari Window" Model). For example, it may be easy for you to honk your horn and wave your fist in the air at the stranger doing something annoying in the car in front of you, but you'd probably be far more forgiving, and less likely to aggress, if that same person doing that annoying thing was your next door neighbour of twenty-five years. What's the difference? You know him...and he knows you, and where you live, too! Relationship, shared history and neighbourly laughs along the way all make you think twice about acting in a way which would damage your years of positive connection. Whether it's the neighbour on your street or the next desk over, the principle remains the same.

The shortest distance between two people is a smile.
— Pianist/Comedian Victor Borge

Share appropriate, funny stories from your personal life to illustrate workplace points and build bonds between teammates. It's amazing how many "outside of work" stories parallel workplace reality and help make a point. To do this you must be *naturally* comfortable with self-disclosure and confessions (that may not always put you in the best light), or learn to get more comfortable with personal information sharing as time goes by.

Of course, humour in the workplace should always be *secondary* to getting the job done efficiently and effectively. The funny thing is (no pun intended), these two goals *can* co-exist. The least costly employer-offered company "benefit" is that of championing and accepting humour in the workplace. When fun is allowed, and humour is an acceptable part of an organization's corporate culture, people *want* to come to work.

> *Any man who has had the job I've had and didn't have a sense of humour wouldn't still be here.*
> — Harry S. Truman

Being against tasteful and appropriately timed humour in the workplace is like being against motherhood. Sometimes, (perhaps because of the stresses of everyday work and life) we know we should embrace more humour in our days, but don't do it. We understand the value of finding the humour in situations, but we don't apply what we say we know. When I find myself saying, "Yeah, yeah, I know, I know, but...". I remind myself, "If I know it but don't do it, I *don't* know it, because if I really *knew* it...I'd *do* it!" Get it? How much do we really know something—understand the concept—if we aren't demonstrating and applying the idea?

As Barbra Streisand sang, in *The Way We Were*, back in 1974, "So it's the laughter we will remember, whenever we remember, the way we were." Ain't it the truth? Lead on and laugh all the way to Friday, each and every week, and all the way to your retirement and beyond!

> *A smile is a curve that sets everything straight.*
> — Phyllis Diller

Taming the Tiger to Access Your Sense of Humour

> *Though a humourist may bomb occasionally, it is still better to exchange humourists than bombs. And...you can't fight when you're laughing.* —Jim Boren

Some people get so triggered (let their "buttons" be pushed) at work, so often, that they seemingly never find their way back to a sense of humour...about anything! How often do *you* let *your* roaring tiger out of the bag at work? How often are you triggered, to the point of anger, by the hundred and one little things that can momentarily knock your day off kilter? Does the anger really help? Do you feel better, afterwards? What's the value in taming your angry "inner tiger" a little more, and keeping your cool in summer, as well as winter, spring and fall?

> *Don't permit yourself to show temper. Always remember that if you are right you can afford to keep your temper, and if you are wrong you cannot afford to lose it!* — J. J. Reynolds

Have you ever been fuming angry at work? I assume your answer is, "Yes". It may feel good to "let 'er rip", but we usually regret our spontaneous lack of professionalism. After all, we'll probably need to interact with the victim of our emotional eruption, another day. A dear friend of mine graphically refers to outwards and noisy expressions of anger as, "emotional vomiting". Granted, not a pretty image, but it does paint a metaphorically accurate picture, doesn't it? So think twice before you surrender to that primitive urge to vent now and pay later, to save your working relationships and also for the good of your own health and well being (as well as that of others).

> *The words you say today should be soft and tender, for tomorrow you may have to eat them.* — Anonymous

Here's what happens when you get "fighting mad":

- you release a quick spurt of adrenalin

- your adrenal glands become enlarged and discoloured

- the lymphatic gland, crucial to the immune system, shrinks intensely

- numerous blood covered ulcers line your stomach

- your cardiovascular system speeds up, breathing rate and heart rate increase by 25%, blood pressure rises and more cholesterol is released into your bloodstream

- chemicals that cause the blood to coagulate are released into your bloodstream to help your body form scabs more easily, in case of injury

- your heart beats more forcefully, perhaps even irregularly

- adrenalin dilates the bronchi to allow a maximum intake of oxygen, as your need for oxygen is momentarily increased

- blood goes from your extremities to your vital organs, leaving your hands and feet cooler and lowering your skin temperature

- your gastrointestinal functioning slows down, sweating increases and your pupils dilate to provide a maximal field of vision

- *all* your senses become more acute; even the patterns of your brain waves change!

When you get *that* angry, your body is fully in "fight or flight" mode—that critical response to stress. If you're going through this kind of strain *daily*, you probably get both emotionally and physically fatigued. It's then that your daily stress and expressed anger causes damage to your personal and professional functioning and productivity.

These physiological changes take two seconds to manifest but up to seventy-two hours to dissipate! Why does this make so many of my audiences laugh right out loud, you may ask? Because they confess that they find *something* to get angry about almost everyday. They never get back to "normal" while they're working. The only time that they actually *do* come back to normal occurs when they:

a)   take vacation
b)   go on stress leave
c)   win the lottery
d)   retire
e)   die, or,
f)   do all of the above!

The Anger Cycle

Nine-tenths of the serious controversies which arise in
life result from misunderstandings. — Louis D. Brandeis

Apply the Anger Cycle to your own experience by thinking of a time when you were *really* angry with a customer, client, colleague, manager or other employee. If you can't think of a work incident, try private life.

Next, draw a circle:

- at the top of your circle, in the twelve o'clock position, write the word "Threat"
- at 3 o'clock put "Assumption"
- at 6 o'clock put "Power Assessment"
- at 9 o'clock put "Anger"

Now...back to your personal anger story. Flash back: you're having a perfectly normal day when, all of a sudden, something happens and you "pop your cork". Remember what triggered your anger? Whether or not you realized it, your anger cycle had begun. First, you experienced a threat. The threat could've been emotional or physical, eg. the emotional threat of someone's disloyalty or not keeping their word, or the physical threat of, say, someone hurling a stapler at you!

In a split second you advanced your anger cycle to the 3 o'clock position by making some negative assumptions about the other's intent. Perhaps thinking something along the lines of, "That dirty, rotten, no good, cheating, lying, bleepity bleep!"

From there, it only took another second to travel to the 6 o'clock spot—the power assessment. Here, usually at a subconscious level, the individual has a heated inner dialogue: "Are you going to let them get away with that? Are you going to let them treat you that way? Talk to you that way? They can't do that to you? Who do they think they are? What are you going to do about it?" Your ego prods you on to strike back with anger. The potentially angry individual reels with thoughts about the degree of power they feel they possess to deal with the situation. While still in the 6 o'clock position on the anger cycle, if the potentially angry person feels power*ful*, they generally move to action, not anger. In such cases, they won't complete the anger cycle. When the potentially angry person feels power*less*, they generally move to anger rather than action; therefore, another quarter turn of the Anger Cycle is travelled.

The 9 o'clock mark on the anger cycle is the *expression* of anger. How did you demonstrate *your* anger in the situation you're recalling for the purpose of this exercise? Some will use a loud voice and cutting words while expressing their anger, others (who feel powerless to directly deal with the threat) will act out varying degrees of passive-aggressive behaviour or snipe with sarcasm, while yet others will turn their anger inwards upon themselves, creating depression. Anger is either explosive/outwards or implosive/inwards. Either way, two or more people are headed for a lose-lose workplace situation once anger starts its spin cycle.

> *Before you embark on a journey of revenge dig two graves.* — Booker T. Washington

Here are some self-talk strategies for breaking the Anger Cycle before it reaches 9 o'clock:

- observe your physiology when you get angry. Listen to your body closely—then you'll be on guard and ready to reconsider your options before you do something you'll regret; if your teeth are clenching, your chest muscles tightening, take ten deep breaths before acting

- ask yourself, "Is this a *real* threat? Am I overreacting? Is this what I'm *really* annoyed about or is this merely the *presenting* issue? What else could it be? What am I *really* angry about?" Dig deeper for some possible answers before travelling to assumptions, at the 3 o'clock mark

- if you *do* travel to assumptions, ask yourself, "Exactly what are my assumptions about this other? Am I sure my assumptions are correct? Could they be faulty? What clarifying questions could I ask before I really lose it?"

- if, after all this, you *still* travel to power assessment, at the 6 o'clock mark, ask yourself, "Am I as powerless as I think? How can I deal with this situation in a positive way? Even if I acknowledge that I'm powerless to effect the result I want, what morsel of powerful thinking or positive self-talk can I own and acknowledge, for the sake of my professional pride and dignity?"

- there may come a time, every now and then, when going the distance with your anger—to the 9 o'clock mark—feels right. Even so, there are still some strategies you can demonstrate which will allow you to be constructive, rather than destructive, in your angry expression. Ask yourself, "Is *now* the right time to express my anger? Am I calm enough to do so, or do I need to take five? What are the benefits of letting it all out? What are the dangers? Is this politically too hot to handle...is it worth it? What assertive (rather than aggressive) words and sentences can I use to express my anger? How can I express my anger while still maintaining the self-esteem and self-confidence of the other? Am I going to feel better or worse, afterwards? Will this matter tomorrow?"

If you do feel the need to take the "Anger Trip" to the very end of the line, here's, perhaps, the best question of all to ask yourself:

- is this situation or issue (over which I'm about to lose emotional balance and serenity) a *preference* or merely a *value*?

Too many of us "go there", regularly, over *preferences*. *Values* are worth sticking up and fighting for, as they're bone deep personal beliefs anchored in family or culture traditions with which we still actively, passionately and consciously agree. *Preferences*, on the other hand, usually muster up much less "fire in the belly"; we may *prefer* something to be this way or that, but we know that we can live with another way, if we must...if we don't "get our own way" on a particular issue. If we must surrender a *preference*, we usually don't loose much sleep over it, but we just might over a *value*. *Preferences* (at least some of them) could be surrendered...for the sake of maintaining ongoing professional relationships and for your own sanity.

"Losing it" multiple times per day, over *preferences*, will keep you hot under the collar in more seasons than just summertime. Conserve your energy for workplace *values* that really matter to you. *By taming* that angry tiger, and *keeping your cool through all the workplace seasons*, you'll only take the most necessary trips on the Anger Cycle, and *that* will allow your humour to surface more often and, in turn, help you to continue to protect your passion for your work.

> *"If you are patient in one moment of anger you will escape one hundred days of sorrow"*.
> — Chinese Proverb

4

Passion Point #4:
Play with Perspective

You must look within for value, but must look beyond for perspective. — Denis Waitley

My first fully conscious hit of the power of perspective and perception occurred while reading my first-year university psychology textbook. The reader was asked to read the following three sentences:

Paris in the	Two peas in a	Pop goes the
the spring	a pod	the weasel

Go ahead. Re-read them aloud for yourself. "What's the big deal," you ask? If you're like most people you probably read, "Paris in the spring; Two peas in a pod; and Pop goes the weasel." Wrong. It says, "Paris in the *the* spring; Two peas in a *a* pod; and Pop goes the *the* weasel". Look at the three sentences again. Do you see what you (probably) missed the first time around? Most everyone misses the second "the" and "a"!

When reading, most people edit what they don't think is relevant. Perhaps this is also true when we experience ourselves and the world around us. Once we think we know everything we need to know, we don't see things that suggest otherwise.

Take an example from private life. Almost everyone has been on one end or the other of this kind of situation: Someone with whom you live is looking for the kitchen scissors (or another oft-misplaced item). He/she asks you where they are. "They're in the second draw beside the stove", you reply. Away goes the other, noisily rummaging through the drawer and, before long, comes back, saying, "They're not there!"

"Yes they are; go back and look again," you reply. Back they go, only to return a minute later, *insisting* the scissors have grown legs and walked away. Mildly exasperated, and quietly looking to the heavens for strength, you abandon what you're doing, march into the kitchen, open the second drawer and...voilà! No scissors. (Don't you just hate it when that happens!) Just kidding. There they are—the scissors! Just as you said!

Was the individual looking for the scissors harassing you? Did he or she decide, "I'll pretend I can't see the scissors, and go back and forth for a couple of rounds, insisting that they're not there, just so that I can see _____ have a minor tantrum."? No. It generally has nothing to do with the person who knows where the scissors are located. It has to do with the individual who, once he or she does not see the scissors, *will* not see them the next time around. For most of us, it's a matter of believing in our ability to observe, understand direction, etc. It's a matter of ego and personal pride. It's "Paris in the the spring; Pop goes the the weasel; and Two peas in a a pod", all over again!

You see what you believe rather than believe what you see. — Dr. Wayne Dwyer

When it comes to examining the parallels between these examples and your own situations, the questions become, "Where in my own life do I stop seeing other possibilities because I think I already have the answers? How stubborn do *I* get in such situations? How does my definition of the right answer, and the fact that I feel I've already found it, potentially squash my ability to think creatively?"

Several years ago I was invited to participate in, "Young

Authors and Career Week", at my daughter's elementary school, at which a selection of children's authors and parents shared what they did for a living. I was delighted to speak to Mrs. Adamo's class of eight and nine year olds (of which my daughter, Kathryn, was a member). As the school was small in numbers, the students of the Grade Four class were very familiar to me. I was well aware of the "popular" kids, the loners, the class clowns and reported "troublemakers".

I hauled out a selection of the fun and tricky exercises with which I typically challenged my adult audiences. And, just like my adult audiences, the children fell into all of the predictable traps. ("Paris in the the spring", yet again!). I shared my adult-style messages about reframing one's perspective. The jury was out as to how well they were drinking it up, until the chief troublemaker, Jeffrey, called my bluff. I challenged the class to count, in unison, from one to ten. Then backwards. Easy enough. The next challenge was to recite the alphabet. Again, easy enough, but I could read in their little faces, "Where is Ms. Spencer going with this, anyway?" Next, the *pièce de résistance*. "OK, now say the alphabet *backwards!*" What Jeffrey did next was priceless.

When I roll out this exercise in front of large audiences, the roar of laughter at the thought of saying the alphabet backwards creates a moment of joviality. Most adults (and children, I discovered, too), will freeze like a deer caught in the headlights and laugh incredulously at the vision of me standing there, waiting for them to begin, "Z, Y, X, W..." Most people think it's a joke and don't even *try* to take on my challenge.

I suggest to my adult audiences (and I also suggested this same possibility to the children), that the reason most people laugh at the idea of reciting the alphabet backwards is that there's no apparent value in learning to do something so silly. Maybe for a parlour game or to be popular at your organization's next picnic, but there isn't any obvious value reciting the alphabet backwards.

Or is there? Studies insist that employees are motivated most by offerings other than monetary reward. Just for fun, and to challenge such findings, I ask my audiences, "If I promised you a million dollars for successfully reciting the alphabet backwards, would you be willing to go out into the hall for an hour and practice? Would it even take you one whole hour to perfect? Most people exuberantly reply that they'd be out of their seats, pronto, and back in 15 minutes having perfected the reversed alphabet. And they say money isn't the biggest motivator—who are they kidding?

My point, here, is this: whether at work or in private life, many ideas or suggestions are deemed impossible, silly or ridiculous, but they can suddenly become worth the effort if the reward and motivation is right.

> You see things; and you say, "Why?" But I dream
> things that never were; and I say, "Why not?"
> — George Bernard Shaw

So let's get back to Mrs. Adamo's class clown. At the challenge of reciting the alphabet backwards, Jeffrey anxiously flailed his fully stretched arm and hand at me, as though hailing a cab, all the while, fidgeting and shouting, "Oh, oh, Ms. Spencer, Ms. Spencer!" Once acknowledged, he promptly jumped to his feet and boasted, "*I* know how to say the alphabet backwards!" Jeffrey's classmates instantly covered their mouths with their hands as they unsuccessfully tried to stifle their giggles, while stealing sideways glances at my daughter with looks that said, "Jeffrey is going to embarrass your mummy!" On top of that, poor Mrs. Adamo, with a look of sudden shock flash-frozen on her face, put her hand on her forehead, shook her head back and forth and slid down into her chair just a little bit. I could tell that she was thinking, "What's Jeffrey going to do? Is he going to embarrass our guest? Can Nina deal with this? Should I step in?" I had no idea what Jeffrey was up to, but I gave both my daughter and Mrs. Adamo a quick smile of reassurance and said, "Come on Jeffrey...let's see what you've got! I'm ready for you!"

Jeffrey swaggered to the front of the class, taking his time for maximum drama, then stood quite erect, puffed up his chest, turned around so that his back was towards the class, and hollered, "A, B, C, D..." *all the while, marching backwards!* Well, Jeffrey's classmates howled with belly laughs, Mrs.

Adamo slunk even further down her chair, and many students stole further sideways glances at my daughter to see how she was taking the fact that Jeffrey had pulled a fast one on her dear old mum. Kathryn was unscathed, knowing that I could make that lemonade out of those lemons!

What did I do? What did I say? My eyes flew open wide, and with the best, gushingly enthusiastic tone of voice I could muster, I congratulated Jeffrey. I congratulated him for his quick and clever thinking. "Do you realize what you've just demonstrated? what you've just proved to yourself and your classmates? You took an idea that most everyone thought was too hard, impossible, silly or ridiculous and then found a way to make it work! I wasn't specific about how to say the alphabet backwards, was I? So your interesting interpretation counts! Do you know what they call this kind of thinking in workplaces, Jeffrey? They call it 'creative thinking', or 'lateral thinking', or 'problem solving', or, to put that more positively, 'solution-oriented'. Employers are looking for the likes of you, Jeffrey. I have a hunch that you'll do just fine when you get into the work world! May I share your example with my audiences from now on?" What could he say? "I dunno...I guess so", came his classic shrugged shoulder response. My presentation was complete. Mrs. Adamo recovered and felt confident to sit up straight in her chair once again and was relieved that I was so good-humoured about her "prize" student's challenge.

P. S. I bumped into teenaged Jeffrey a couple of years ago and told him that his actions that day, and my recounting of them with current day audiences, are *still* inspiring people to rethink what is "doable" if you're motivated and willing to reframe your perspective. Of course, and as you probably guessed, he rolled his eyes with mock embarrassment...*and* a little smile. Forever the charming devil. Who'd have thought that the "troublemaker" of the group would be the one with such a powerful piece of wisdom? Even *that* turns out to be a new perspective on the quintessential class clown stereotype! Does such a person exist in your workplace, perhaps?

It Couldn't Be Done

Somebody said it couldn't be done,
But he with a chuckle replied
That "maybe it couldn't," but he would be one
Who wouldn't say so till he tried.
So he buckled right in with a trace of a grin
On his face. If he worried he hid it.
He started to sing as he tackled the thing
That couldn't be done and he did it.

Somebody scoffed, "Oh you'll never do that;
At least no one ever has done it."
But he took off his coat and he took off his hat
And the first thing we knew he'd begun it.
With a lift of his chin and a bit of a grin,
Without any doubting or quiddit
He started to sing as he tackled the thing
That couldn't be done and he did it.

There are thousands to tell you it cannot be done;
There are thousands to prophesy failure;
There are thousands to point out to you one by one,
The dangers that wait to assail you.
But just buckle in with a bit of a grin,
Just take off your coat and go to it;
Just start to sing as you tackle the thing
That "cannot be done" and you'll do it.

— Edgar A. Guest

Here's yet another example of just how competent we can be at seeing different perspectives if we decide to give ourselves permission. Read the following aloud:

The Paomnhehal Pweor of the Hmaun Mnid!

"I cdnuolt blveiee that I cluod aulaclty uesdnatnrd what I was rdeniag. Aoccdrnig to a rscheearch study at Cmabrigde Uinervtisy, it deosn't Mttaer in what order the ltteers in a word are, the only iprmoatnt thing Is that the frist and lsat ltteer be in the rghit pclae. The rset can be a taotl mess and you can still raed it wouthit porbelm. This is bcuseae the human mind deos not raed ervey lteter by istlef, but the word as a wlohe. Amzanig huh? (as originally appeared in the *Cambridge On-line News*, U.K., August 16, 2003). That really *is* pretty amazing, isn't it? Did you feel yourself getting puffed up with pride and confidence at *your* brainpower while reading this passage?

Here's one last piece of fun that helps illustrate the power of playing around with perspective...it came to me while flipping through a magazine one day. The advertisement described:

"Pan grilled bread stuffed with a blend of three cheeses, complemented with strips of fresh carrot and celery and beans simmered in a sauce of tomatoes and fine spices."

To what was this elegantly worded advertisement referring? Grilled cheese with baked beans! Heinz's clever closing line in this ad? "And *you* thought they were just beans." Ahhh the power of the right words to change a perspective!

Perspective and Control

> *When we are no longer able to change a situation, we are challenged to change ourselves.* — Victor Frankl

Perspective has everything to do with how you think about control. Consider these four questions, and write down your thoughts:

- *Who* do I control?

- Who *don't* I control?

- *What* do I control?

- What *don't* I control?

Do this exercise for yourself; try it with your team, too. Examine and compare your answers. Do you see a pattern? Most people note the things they can't control—weather, traffic, a colleague's mood swings, a difficult customer, etc.—are things *outside of* themselves. If only your life came with a built-in remote control, *then* you *could* control another. Just imagine...you could put someone on pause while you thought of a clever rebuttal. You could even "mute" someone, rewind them, or turn them off altogether! If only, if only...too bad that's not real life!

You may *not* be able to actually control another, all of your workplace circumstances or even some of the moods you embrace (let's face it, whether it's the utmost joy or the angriest fury you've ever experienced, for most, it's hard to get any well defined mood to last much longer than about 15 minutes!), but you *can* demonstrate and develop your ability to *influence, persuade and inspire (IPI)*. I don't mean you should learn to be manipulative, but, rather, learn to develop a high level of competency and expertise at interpersonal communications. All fine leaders are good at this, and they know how to do it *on purpose and by design*—not just by an accident of good character or by nature. The IPI skills, like all skills, are amoral. You can learn how to influence, persuade and inspire others to do *bad* or you can apply these same skills to do *good*. Your personal motivation and goals are the key. Think of control like the weather...when you go outside you get whatever's there. It's up to you to modify your perspective so you can deal with all the "weather", workplace or otherwise, successfully.

> *Arrange whatever pieces come your way.*
> — Virginia Woolf

What situations in your work and/or private life need reframing? What do you bellyache about so much that you even bore *yourself* at times? Do you sometimes feel trapped by the *paralysis of analysis* of a situation?

Even though you intellectually understand the process of changing your perspective, for some reason, it sometimes seems hard to do. In such cases, ask yourself, "What's the pay off for me for holding on to *this* perspective? What is it that I get to *keep*, tangible or otherwise, if I hold on to this perspective? What do I think will happen if I shift my perspective—good or bad? Is it possible that, by shifting perspective around this particular situation, I might experience more peace, happiness, harmony, satisfaction or even learn a profound life lesson? If you can learn the skill of facilitating yourself through these types of introspective/reflective questions while in the actual moment of struggle, all the more power to you–literally.

In the late 1990's and early into the 2000's I visited my extended family in England most every summer, especially because my maternal grandmother was fast approaching her 100th birthday (she since passed away on New Year's Day, 2004, just a few months short of her 100th birthday). Now *that's* another example of perspective...on the importance of making the most of one's time. I believe it was Andy Rooney who said that, "Life is like a roll of toilet paper—it goes faster when you get near the end of the roll!" When distant friends and family are young and in good health, the urgency to visit is often reduced; when they're aged, you'd better hurry up because any day could be their last. The reality, of course, is that this is true all through our lives; we just don't seem to notice so much, when we're under 30 or 40.

Although when I visited England our number one priority was Nana, we always squeezed in some sightseeing. There are few cities in the world that offer up as many wonderful sights as London and vicinity (but I may be prejudiced here)! It was during the summer of 2001, on the way to Greenwich to visit The Royal Observatory and straddle one foot on either side of the line marking the Prime Meridian, that a little boat on the River Thames offered up one of my most profound lessons on perspective.

The Thames, during the summer months, attracts scads of sightseeing boat tours. On this particularly sunny July day, the wide, choppy river was throbbing and bobbing with large and small tour boats. Some were very grand, all white and glistening, multi-tiered and very modern and clean looking. Sort of like the *Love Boat*. Some were smaller. We purchased our tickets from what we thought was the central wicket for *all* tour boats, to cruise 40 minutes down the Thames, from Westminster Bridge (in the heart of London, overlooking the Houses of Parliament and "Big Ben") to Greenwich. We lined up dockside and waited to climb aboard. What a cruel joke some-one had played on us all. The beautiful multi-tiered boat with the open upper deck slowed down and then sailed right on past our dock and on to the next. In its wake, the boat of *my* unfortunate destiny chugged along, spewing what smelled like kerosene behind! What were we to do? We'd already bought our tickets. As this smelly, antiquated, fully enclosed, one level boat came alongside the dock, it was hard to hide my disappointment. For me, the 40-minute boat ride with Canary Wharf on the right and St. Paul's Cathedral on the left and London's famous Tower Bridge straight ahead was to be part of the joy. Now what was I going to do?

With my first step aboard this seemingly floating death trap, named the Hurlingham, I secretly and melodramatically feared for my life. We found our way to a collection of flimsy, plastic, stackable chairs that had seen better days. Once seated, I felt as though my line of sight was level with the water. It was pretty low down compared to "The Love Boat", upon which I would not sail. I scanned the interior for life preservers and made a mental note of their location, just in case. As we pulled away from shore, and for many minutes after, all my pearls of professional wisdom and advice fell from my thoughts. In those moments, I certainly was *not* practicing what I preached from the speaker's platform. I confess, my preoccupation with the doubtful sea-worthiness of my vessel, along with its chintzy interior, robbed me of the pleasure of this leg of our excursion. This, despite the fact that our Cockney-accented tour guide (who, by the way, also doubled as the *captain* of the boat), tried his hardest to be funny, in a cynical and sarcastic way. Under other circumstances I would've laughed along, but not this day; this poor fellow, doing his best with what he had to work, only inflamed my annoyance, until...

Two thirds of the way to our destination, the captain piped up with, "Some of you may wonder about the history of this boat." ("No kidding", I snickered.) "Well", he carried on, "It's the oldest working boat still in operation on the Thames, dating to before World War Two." (Why was I *not* surprised?) "It's not as fancy as some of the other boats carrying you tourists to and fro along the river, to be sure, but it has at least one thing over all those other boats that makes it the pride and joy of the Thames." "Do tell...pleeease!", I muttered, sarcastically to my aunt.

Well, try he did...and succeeded...in *spades!* "This little boat was the saviour of hundreds of British and Allied Soldiers stranded at Dunkirk" (the French port on the English Channel, which was the scene of the evacuation of the British Expeditionary Force in 1940; in the early days of WWII they were forced to retreat by the German breakthrough at Sedan; 335,000 British and Allied forces were evacuated from the shores of Dunkirk between May 27 and June 2 by warships, requisitioned civilian ships, and a host of small boats just like the one I was on, all the while under constant attack from the air). Wow! Now *that* made everything different! ("Why didn't you say so!")

In a nanosecond I went from smoldering contempt for this cavernous workhorse of a vessel to one of reverent awe. I now heard the echoes of the relieved and grateful ghosts of the troops who had been spared on those dark days in 1940, thanks to, among others, this "little boat that could". The captain continued, "And it made *three* return crossings!" Old softy that I am, the tears flowed from my eyes. Somewhat embarrassed, as I fished around my purse for a tissue (while wondering why only my aunt and I were blubbering), I realized, "I've got to get a picture...I've *got* to take a picture of me with this oh-so-special vessel!" So there we were, my aunt and I, standing by the shiny commemorative brass plaque which read, "Dunkirk 1940"; that same plaque that had been there all along (and for over sixty years!), which I—with my blinders firmly in place—neglected to see upon boarding.

We don't see things as they are, we see them as we are.
— Anais Nin

Maximize the powerful lessons to be learned from the practice of raising your conscious awareness and reframing perspective by watching out for the lessons in the seemingly little and insignificant mundane events of everyday life. These lessons are there for the taking if we would only slow down and interpret our observations.

One of my most recent personal lessons in framing perspective was presented to me in the ladies washroom (of all places) moments before I was due to deliver a keynote address. With just moments to spare, and nature urgently calling, I hurried into the facilities and pushed on the door of one of the cubicles. It was locked! So I tried the next; it too was locked. On I went to the next, and yet the next. They were all locked! I bent over, to look for feet, but I was alone. Anxiously, I pushed on one particular door two or three more times. Nothing.

Exasperated, and surrendering to the fact that all the cubicle doors were locked for some reason (perhaps a plumbing problem?), and now, with very little time to spare, I started to leave, in search of another washroom. Just as my hand was on the exit, I saw, out of the corner of my eye, that *all* the cubicle doors had slightly opened! Was I on some new reality TV show? No. I immediately laughed at myself, and shook my head in wonder at my narrow thinking as the explanation became immediately apparent. The doors opened by *pulling* rather than pushing. When was the last time washroom doors were designed *that* way (with the exception of wheelchair access ones, of course)? Never-the-less, that's the way all of these particular doors were installed. I thought to myself, "Tisk, tisk, Nina...you *teach* this stuff. You were so anxious and in a hurry to get back to the ballroom that you didn't slow down enough to consider the perspective of *pulling* instead of pushing! You automatically assumed that there was only one way to move forth and you willfully kept *pushing* for it, literally and metaphorically, to no avail. Now where's the lesson in this for you? How does this apply to your life?" I answered my own question immediately.

> *When one door closes, another opens; but we often look so long and so regretfully upon the closed door that we do not see the ones which open for us.*
> — Alexander Graham Bell

If we insist on moving forth with *one* strategy to successfully complete a task, and we meet resistance, pushing some more, in exactly the same way, is hardly likely to yield results. Sometimes, rather than using force and willfulness to get more of what we want, it just may be more effective to back off and "trust the process". Do *you* recall a time when you, too, tried too hard, either personally or professionally, and got nowhere, and then later that very same day, or sometime soon after, when you relaxed or shifted your perspective, found the results you were seeking came to you without effort? It's that old expression all over again: "If I always do what I've always done, I'll always get what I've always got."

If you want to get something different, you have to *do* something different! Constantly reminding yourself to reframe, reframe, reframe your perspective, can be that lovely passkey to moving forth with your ideas, desires and dreams... all of which can help lead you back to your passion for your profession.

5

Putting Purpose into Your Daily Professional Practice

> *If you can't do great things, do small things in a great way. Don't wait for great opportunities. Seize common, everyday ones and make them great.*
> — Napolean Hill

Have you ever asked yourself why you do the job you do? It's easy to come up with quick answers—to pay the mortgage/rent, go on vacations, support the kids' education—but you could do *that* in any number of jobs. You work hard in your current position for more reasons than the fact that it pays the bills. Otherwise, you'd probably have already moved on to your next professional opportunity. Still, on some of those truly awful days at work, most everyone has asked themselves, "*Why* do I do this job? *Why* am I staying here?"

It's easier to stay the course on bad days when you know *why* you're doing what you're doing. That's why getting clear about your bigger picture purpose is so helpful for sustaining passion for your profession. Try author Peter Senge's "Five Whys" test. Ask yourself, five times, "Why do I do this job?" and for each answer, ask, "And why is *that* important to me?" By the time you get to the fifth "Why" you'll probably have something that sounds a lot like the *real* reason you do the work you do. Articulating a sense of purpose can help you through the worst workplace doldrums and difficult situations, and also help keep you passionate for the good work you perform.

> *Trusting my value system can be a major contribution to my work.* — Anne Wilson Schaef

You can bring a feeling of personal passion to even the most modest of frontline professions if you're clear about *why* you do it. Values clarification exercises are a classic way to begin gaining clarity of purpose.

Here's a quick exercise to get you started. Look at this selection of personal values. Add additional ones if you wish. Place a check mark beside those values you personally embrace, an "X" beside those you disregard and a "?" beside those to which you're ambivalent:

_____ Professional success

_____ Honesty and authenticity

_____ Religious involvement and practice

_____ Social appropriateness

_____ Open mindedness

_____ A strong sense of individuality

_____ Workplace autonomy

_____ Winning

_____ Family success

_____ Giving my children a competitive advantage

_____ Being a law abiding citizen

_____ Loyalty to my country

_____ Loyalty to my sub-culture

____ Organized home life

____ Keeping commitments

____ Knowing the right contacts and people

____ Work/life balance

____ Having many friends

____ Having a diversity of friends

____ Being multi-skilled

____ Efficient, prepared and calm during emergencies

____ Athletic competencies

____ Community, region, and/or country pride

____ Musicality

____ Awareness of my family history and sub-cultural heritage

____ Presenting the right image/social etiquette

____ Honouring my parents/taking care of my parents

____ Ability to build things/work with my hands

____ Thrift/frugality

____ Financial wealth

____ Self-sufficiency/independence

____ Involvement with government

____ Marital success and happiness

____ Fame or highly profiled public acknowledgement
        within my profession/my work

____ Personal productivity

____ Personal creativity

_____ Serving the less fortunate/volunteerism/ donating to charities

_____ Health and wellness

_____ Keeping careful personal and professional records

_____ Appreciating and embracing other cultures

_____ Demonstrating my personal leadership

_____ Mentoring others, in both my personal and professional lives

_____ Continuous learning/personal and professional growth

_____ Faith in God/highly developed sense of spirituality

_____ Financial security for now and for retirement

_____ Personal attractiveness/physical beauty

_____ Tolerance and acceptance of others

_____ Being witty, quick, clever and articulate

_____ Artistic appreciation

_____ Being a good team player

_____ Dressing for success

_____ Skill to influence, persuade and inspire

_____ Skill to repair things, solve problems, find solutions

_____ Accuracy of work

_____ Strong discipline and focus on desired tasks and beliefs

Of these values that you embrace (those marked with an check mark), choose the four most important to you. Now review those that you disregard or reject (those marked with an "X"). Of these selections, which four are of the *least* important to you? Consider and compare your top four values with your four most disregarded. Note whether you spend your working days moving towards, or away from, your four most important values. Do you experience congruency between your four most cherished values and your daily workplace activities, attitudes and behaviours? How much personal energy, time, effort and talent do you expend on any given workday to values you *reject?*

If your honest answer is not to your liking, you may be experiencing personal "values conflicts" in your work. And if that's the case, the conflicts may be standing in the way of accessing your deep professional purpose, and of gaining or regaining passion for your profession. If that's so, further exploration of your values and goals may be a good idea.

It concerns us to know the purposes we seek in life, for then, like archers aiming at a definite mark, we shall be more likely to attain what we want. — Aristotle

To examine professional purpose sincerely (or personal/life purpose, too), first explore and identify your personal values. This can be accomplished in a number of ways. The first and simplest of ways is to put yourself through some values clarification exercises and inventories (like the ones you've just completed). It's essential to hold a clear set of personal values to determine and articulate a professional purpose. Without a clear understanding of one's personal values it becomes easy to *react* to situations (particularly difficult ones), rather than *respond* in ways that are more personally meaningful and purposeful.

Values-clarifying exercises can be challenging. They often take quite a bit of musing, self-assessment and introspection, and that's why most people don't bother. Most people don't want to think that hard! They take you away from the easier, autopilot activities of everyday life—but it *is* worth the effort.

Values planning and identification is a long and dynamic process on the way to understanding and declaring (even if it's only to yourself) your professional purpose. It takes longer than twenty minutes to successfully and deeply complete. Values clarification and conviction is a journey with many opportunities to re-examine, re-visit and re-define as years go by...and

life has a funny way of forcing us to rethink our most important values, especially when adversity comes to call! This
process of selecting those values you embrace versus those you
reject is a start, but the real value of doing this work comes
from hours, weeks, months and years of commitment to creating more and more alignment between your clearly identified
and articulated values and the work you do. From this, your
personal purpose can spring forth.

> *Your work is to discover your work and then with all
> your heart to give yourself to it.* — Buddha

**Here's another quick exercise to get you thinking about, and articulat-
ing, your professional purpose. To sustain passion for your profession,
and to get clearer about professional purpose, answer these questions:**

1. What do I want from my work/my job?
2. What do I want my job to give me/do for me?
3. What do I want to experience because of my work
    contribution?
4. What product or service does my organization provide?
5. How does my corner of the organization, and my job in
    particular, connect to the product or service my organiza-
    tion provides? how does my contribution help it happen?
6. How does my organization's product or service benefit the
    client?
7. How does that benefit to the client, plug into my personal
    value system?
8. Who is my primary client, anyway? secondary? other?
9. Am I proud to be part of my organization and what it
    provides?
10. What can I do to create even more congruence between
    my organization's values and my own?

> *Give me an occupation...or I shall run mad.*
> —Character Colonel Brandon from
> Jane Austen's *Sense and Sensibility*

Your job may be *part* of your purpose, but the job, in and of itself, is *not* your purpose...it's the daily vehicle or conduit through which you get to fulfill your purpose. And once you articulate your professional purpose, you'll find that it's overarching enough to carry you through *any* professional position you may hold from now until retirement and beyond. To explore this issue further, I suggest *The Path: Creating Your Mission Statement for Work and for Life*, by Laurie Beth Jones. It's a terrific book for delving deeper into personal values assessment, vision, goals and, ultimately, personal life mission statements.

Your work either elevates your sense of life or stifles it. To feel positive and passionate for your work, no matter where you are on the organizational ladder, it helps abundantly to find alignment between *what you do and what you value*. The bottom line is this: your work either moves you *closer* to your best, higher self, or keeps you from it.

Every moment of one's existence, one is growing into more or retreating into less. One is always living a little more or dying a little bit. — Norman Mailer

6

Passion Point #6:
Preserve Your Energy and Enthusiasm

*Age may wrinkle the face, but lack of enthusiasm
wrinkles the soul.* — Samuel Ulman

What comes first...energy or enthusiasm? It could be argued that physical and emotional energy fuel enthusiasm. On the other hand, enthusiasm is often the burst of *gusto* needed to get up and go with your energy. Think back to the last time you thought you had no energy to do *anything* (perhaps at the end of a long and trying day). Imagine a friend calls offering you tickets to tonight's long ago sold-out concert by your favourite recording artist. Wouldn't you be ready to go in an hour? Wouldn't you be astonished at the "emergency" store of energy you discovered within yourself?

Think...what came first? Enthusiasm! What came next? Energy! The energy to get up off the couch, get dressed and get out of the house, *quick*. All done with reserves of energy you didn't know you had a few moments beforehand. It doesn't matter which spurs the other. They're both important to feeling passion for your daily work. And, of course, energy and enthusiasm are both close cousins of purpose, humour, professional self-worth and positive thinking. They *all* hang together for the best passionate results.

Have you ever noticed that when some people show up at work the energy level goes up? They're usually upbeat, charismatic people, easy to like and regularly make a positive contribution. I call these people, "energy angels".

Others show up and the energy goes down, down, down. You can almost hear "whoosh...thud" as the energy gets sucked out of the room. I call *them*, "energy vampires". Under which category do you fall?

> *Take charge of your own energy and then help orchestrate the energy of those around you.* — Peter Drucker

Energy vampires are like the office porcupines I discussed earlier, in the chapter on humour. Energy suckers may not consciously mean to be negative, but that's how others experience them. Can the porcupines be turned around? Perhaps. It depends how serious and deep the issues run that cause them to be miserable, in the first place. It also depends on their desire to do something about it. Regardless, even if you're magnanimous and kinder than most to crabby colleagues, it's essential that you *protect your own energy*. When it comes to protecting your own energy, I often recommend *Star Trek Next Generation's* "shields up!" strategy. When entering the "space" of an energy vampire remember to command "shields up" so their contaminants don't seep into your thinking. You must have a purposeful attitudinal defense to protect yourself from such negative individuals, otherwise, without even knowing, they will win you over to their disagreeable side in no time flat.

It's hard to work side-by-side with negative energy, day-in and day-out, without succumbing some of the time. You'd think that ten people on a team would each hold one tenth of the team's energy and disposition, but that's not always the case. Sometimes *one or two* individuals wield more influence over the team's health and productivity than one would ever expect. Sometimes *one* negative team member's contamination can damage the other nine people's contributions and efforts. It's like making lemon meringue pie. You beat the whites of eggs to create the stiff peaks crowning the pie. But if there's one *smidgeon* of yolk in the egg whites—one little dot of contaminant—the eggs whites won't whip up into the anticipated peaks no matter how much you beat them. And there won't be any pie for anyone. (Not that I'm suggesting you beat your negative colleagues into shape!). As much as possible, for a team to be truly successful and maximally productive, it must be "pure" and without the "contaminant" of the negative influence.

To help both yourself and your team "make it", take care of your physical *and* emotional energy by starting (or sustaining) your commitment to take care of yourself. Contribute to the *positive* (not the negative) physical and emotional energy of your workplace. Your efforts *will* make a difference.

Recognize the Links Between Attitude, Desserts and Living in the "New Normal".

Shortly after September 11, 2001, the Canadian national newspaper, *The Globe and Mail*, in conjunction with CTV and Ipsos-Reid pollsters, conducted an opinion poll. The *Globe* subsequently covered the results using headlines such as:

"Work Life Stress Mounting for Canadians"

"Canadians Feeling Weight of the World"

"Tension between Work and Home Growing"

"Fighting the Fear Factor: How Can We Cope?"

"Poll Finds Rising Stress and Fear in Canada"

The post-9/11 report noted that one in four Canadians always or often felt stressed since September 11th. One in three were more anxious and irritable than normal. Another poll, conducted by the Heart and Stroke Foundation, reported that two thirds of Canadians feared more for their personal safety and that of their families, and 57% were experiencing "severe or significant stress since the terror campaign began".

These headlines specifically related to how Canadians were feeling immediately after 9/11, but take a look at the titles again...could they not appear in today's newspapers as well? Now and again, newspapers around the western world continue to write about the exorbitant costs of workplace stress to employee well being, organizational productivity and bottom line results.

On-the-job stress has been a subject of conversation (and professional development workshops, too!) for at least the past decade. This isn't new. What *is* new is that larger numbers of employees are working with increasing stress levels and for prolonged periods of time. Stressed employees impact workplace results and squash staff energy and enthusiasm. How can you possibly access lightheartedness and hopeful, positive expression when there's such a feeling of gloom and despair in the workplace air? *That* is the question!

Now that you think about it...are these good days or bad days for you at work? Are you and your fellow employees more anxious and irritable these days? Do you/they have shorter fuses? How is that impacting customer service and inter-departmental communications? If employees are having trouble sleeping, they may be fatigued, inaccurate and make poor decisions. How much room for error is there in the product or service your organization provides?

There's a growing body of research that shows a direct link between stress and physical health, which leads to lost productivity and absenteeism. What have you noticed in your own organization over the past few years? Is it "business as usual" now or have things seemed at least a little different—more strained, anxious, tender or uncertain?

> *When you get to the end of your rope, tie a knot and hang on.* — Franlklin D. Roosevelt

Here are six simple, cost-efficient strategies to keep it together at work:

1. **Drink...water, that is!** Drink six to eight glasses of room temperature water, or a little warmer, daily. Yes, yes, I've heard it all before. "It's too *hard* to get eight glasses of water in me!" Well, guess what? It *can* be done without having to make a pit stop on the way to work every morning; here's how:

   Step 1. Get out of bed.

   Step 2. Go to the washroom.

   Step 3. Drink two eight ounce glasses of water *in a row*— there you go, down the hatch! I suggest tepid or warm water because it slides down the gullet easier, especially in the morning. On top of that, it's not as shocking to your system right after you've been warm and snuggly all night. You must have these two glasses right after you get up so they can work their way through your system before you leave for work. The trick here is to make sure you "go" before you leave the house...just like your mummy used to tell you. (I can't believe I'm coaching "potty" strategies in a business book!)

Step 4. Grab two more glasses as soon as you arrive at work—assuming that you'll have access to facilities an hour or so later, and that you won't be stuck in a meeting from which you can't excuse yourself. Now you're up to four glasses and it's not yet even noon!

Step 5. Have yourself another glass of tepid water with your lunch.

Step 6. Drink another at afternoon break (if there's such a thing in your work day), and then lay off until you get home. So far you're already up to six!

Step 7. Reach for your seventh of the day the moment you're home.

Step. 8. Take your last and eighth glass of the day at least 90 minutes before bedtime. There you go—eight glasses, one day. Voilà! You'll never be thirsty all day long, ever again. Give it a try. I promise you it works, and it's so, so good for you for so many reasons! Here's one of those reasons...distracting, mid-afternoon headaches are often caused by fatigue brought on by dehydration. Drink your water *before* you're pained and parched. By the time you're so thirsty that you've just *gotta hava drink*, it's too late; you're already dehydrated (and reaching for the aspirin bottle, to boot).

2. Come together: Bring your team together for some light hearted bonding. How about a year end/festive team breakfast? Team lunches run long and interrupt your stride. A team *breakfast* can invigorate and energize your team for the entire day!

3. **Talk about anything except local and/or world news tragedies, for one whole day!** I found myself talking about the "War on Terrorism" every dinnertime immediately after September 11, 2001. It took my then-15 year old daughter to say, "Mum, you've talked about this every day this week. Can we pleeease have *one* meal together where we talk about *anything* else?" It wasn't that she didn't have concern or compassion about world events...she just needed a few moments *off* to regroup her energy so that she could be of value and make a contribution later (as did we all, I suspect, whether or not we realized it).

4. **Sing with gusto.** Research shows that singing shifts the emotions and reduces fear. It helps focus our thoughts on things other than worry and stress. The de-stressing power of music is so important that some major hospitals staff full-time music therapists. The next time you're on your way to work, bring along your favourite songs. Provided you're in the privacy of a car, sing your songs out loud...with gusto! Yeah, someone might see you (but they won't *hear* you) and they won't even see you if *you* don't look to see if they're looking—you know what I mean? By the time you arrive at work you'll feel absolutely exhilarated. You may even have those uplifting lyrics running through your head the entire day, keeping you motivated.

5. **Decide to be kinder with coworkers, customers, neighbours, friends and family.** Many of us wear our professional face all day long, and then, when we come home, spout our first irritable words of the day before we're even out of the front hall. A few years ago a little piece of serendipity happened for me. I use a lot of small, happy-face stickers for reminders of this and that. One of these stickers mysteriously landed on the threshold of my front door. As I went to remove it, that happy face looked up at me. I thought about the "coincidence" of this sticker being at my doorstep...that symbol of transition from "work life" to "family life". My intuition told me to leave it there, to act as a reminder to give the very same "best" to my *family*

that I easily and cheerfully give to my clients. It's been there ever since. That now very dirty little golden-faced symbol has reminded me, many times over the years, of how I want to be and act with my loved ones in the next moment, as I cross the threshold into my home at the end of any given day. Plant your own symbols at work and home (and even in your car) to remind you of how you want to be and act. External reminders help...especially if we're so stressed we're not thinking with our "higher brains".

6. **Practice positive self-talk: optimistic and positively focused people frequently use negative words without even knowing it!** I first addressed this strategy in Chapter One. To reinforce this concept, once again, remember to ask yourself, "Do I express what I *do* want by articulating what I *don't?*" If you must confess, "Yup...I'm guilty of this", you're using negative talk. You're using it with others and you're probably using it on yourself, too. As I pointed out in Chapter One, remember to use *positive* thinking, language and word choice wherever possible, eg. "Have I caught you at a bad time?" draws attention to the idea and visceral feeling of "bad time". Use the positive alternative of, "Have I got you at a *good* time?" Find dozens of ways and excuses, each and every day to couch your words in a more positive way. When you catch yourself using the negative, immediately correct and counter with the positive alternative. Before you know it, positive word choices will be coming out of your mouth automatically and forever more.

We all have the capacity to choose and direct ourselves to be more peaceful and positively focused. These six simple strategies can make a terrific contribution. Too difficult to implement, some may say? Consider these sage words:

> *It is not because things are difficult that we do not dare; it is because we do not dare that things are difficult. —* Seneca

And just what are those links between attitude, desserts and the "new normal" (which I mentioned near the beginning of this chapter), you may ask?

Well...if you create a numeric equivalent for each letter of "A-T-T-I-T-U-D-E" (example, where A = 1, T = 20), the word "Attitude" equals 100. Desserts are delicious and most people would rather have them than not! "Desserts" reversed is "stressed". Who figures these things out, anyway? I confess to say, it wasn't me! In which direction would *you* rather go...to *desserts* or *stressed*? And the "new normal" merely is what it is—welcome to it. So here are the links, as I see them: it takes 100% of your positive, focused *attitude*, effort and commitment to choose desserts over being *stressed*, to successfully work and live in the "new normal". Do yourself and those around you a big favour and treat yourself to a metaphoric, or even literal, decadent dozen fine quality truffles! Now *there's* a dessert! Now, more than ever, you probably deserve it!

> *Enthusiasm is one of the most powerful engines of success. When you do a thing, do it with all your might...be active, be energetic, be enthusiastic and faithful, and you will accomplish your objective.*
>
> — Ralph Waldo Emerson

7

Passion Point #7:
Promise to Persevere

We must not hope to be mowers,
And to gather the ripe gold ears,
Unless we have first been sowers
And watered the furrows with tears.
It is not just as we take it,
This mystical world of ours,
Life's field will yield as we make it
A harvest of thorns or of flowers.

– Johann Wolfgang Goethe

"Persevere", according to the *Oxford English Reference Dictionary* means, "to continue steadfastly or determinedly." *Chambers Dictionary of Etymology: The Origins and Development of Over 25,000 English Words*, says this word comes from Old French, and before that, from Latin, and means, "continue steadfastly, abide by, persist". Chambers also provides the psychological definition: "The tendency to continue or repeat an action after the need or stimulus has passed."

When you have fire in your belly, your purpose is clear, your mental and physical energy is strong, and you know your professional worth...the underpinning of it all, to sustain your passion and balance through the dark hours of the soul, is *perseverance*.

You may be in the right job, and in the right profession and organization, too, and *still* get into a funk from time-to-time. *Cut yourself some slack and persevere.* Blue periods disappear sooner or later. Learn to keep the faith. Let me share my own, most vivid "blue period/keep the faith" work story with you.

A Personal Story of Professional Perseverance

Never give up, for that is just the place and time that the tide will turn. — Harriet Beecher Stowe

I started into the independent/entrepreneurial phase of my professional speaking life, many years ago now, in a January. I was both delighted and encouraged by the number of engagements I secured during that first twelve months. December of my first year was busy with both personal and professional events and was full of typical (at least for me) holiday indulgence and year-end spending. When January rolled around once again, marking my first complete year in business for myself, my office phone was silent....during the first week, then the second...and then even the third! And *then*...the January bills started to arrive (and we all know what that's like!).

One particular day, multiple bills arrived. As I sat in my office, quietly contemplating my momentarily modest bank balance and wondering what was to be done, my lower lip began to quiver. Before I knew it I was having a good cry. My husband, down the hall in his own office, came rushing to see what was the matter. I blubbered, "My bills are mounting and my business cash flow is dwindling to the point where I'm feeling so nervous about it all. Why did I leave corporate life? Why did I think I could make a go of it? What was I thinking? I don't have any engagements booked until the end of March and my phone's not ringing! I can't take this financial emotional rollercoaster anymore. What am I going to do?"

My husband reminded me I'd had a fabulous first year, with terrific client feedback, and that I had every reason to believe the second would be even better. All I had to do, he encouraged, was keep the faith and believe in myself. I was too emotional, in that moment, to really listen or pay heed to his words (and too busy looking for a tissue to wipe away my tears and dribbling nose), so he continued, "Just keep doing what you're doing...the follow-ups, the prospecting new opportunities, developing your topics and materials...you'll see...the phone will ring—I promise you!" Well who'd have thunk; the phone *did* ring...that very second. It was like a scene from an over-staged and predictable production. I panicked. How could I answer the phone now...all stuffy and snotty sounding and so emotionally low? "Answer the phone!", my husband insisted. "I can't". "Yes you can...answer it! I can't!!" "Nina...answer it now before it jumps over to voice mail!" "OK, OK, I will." And I did. Amazingly, some how I stopped my "water works" on a dime, picked up the phone at the end of the last ring, and with my best "fake it 'til you make it" sunny voice and disposition, answered, "Good afternoon, Nina Spencer speaking". Who was the caller, you may wonder? It was a potential client, with whom I'd been "dancing" for months. They'd finally decided, now that it was a new year and now that everyone had recovered from "holiday hangovers", to book my services for *four* full day workshops and, "Oh, by the way... could you possibly deliver all of them before the end of February?" They hadn't even suspected that only a couple of minutes earlier I was a blubbering mess. I hung up the phone a changed woman. "See", my husband chided, "you didn't need to get to the point of tears and spend all that energy fretting, after all, did you?" He was right.

P. S. Later that day, I recounted this whole event to another dear family member. His response was, "See, you should cry more often; it made the phone ring!" There you go. I offer up this story as my personal example of hanging on and persevering through professionally rough patches, but the "P. S." comments of my other family member could also cause this little ditty to be a "Perspective" or "Positive versus Negative Thinking" story, as well. Do you agree? And as for me, I remind myself of this particular perseverance experience anytime even a 1% smidgeon of doubt comes knocking at my professional door (remember the damage a 1% contaminate can make to that lemon merengue pie?).

Sometimes things arrive in their own mysterious hour, on their own terms and not yours, to be seized or relinquished forever. — Gail Godwin

Cut Yourself Some Slack and Lighten Up

Write on your heart that every day is the best day of the year. — Ralph Waldo Emerson

What strategies do *you* employ to push through emotional rough spots at work, to continue steadfastly or repeat a positively focused action in the face of a "blue" stimulus? Next time you feel yourself about to take a ride on the "big blue slide", make a list of the things that you love about your work (and keep it close by to look at every now and then). Try shining a little "light" on the situation!

Here is my spin on six "lighten-up" insights and thoughts (inspired by humourist Loretta Laroche's video, *Humour Your Stress: Jest for the Fun of it*):

- **Lighten Up Your Heart:** find some humour in everyday workplace challenges; laugh at yourself, as well. Sometimes we all take ourselves so seriously. Read some of the jokes friends email you. You might even decide, every once in a while, to pass along a particularly funny one to a colleague you know is going through a difficult time (even though you swear up and down that you usually don't send this kind of "stuff").

- **Light the Way for Others:** one of the best ways to get over your own pity party is to focus on someone else's needs. Who can you connect with whom? How can you be the conduit who brings two good people together? A couple of summers ago I spoke at an international conference, after which a participant from Ghana contacted me, enquiring about professional services that weren't quite up my alley. I could have delivered a competent package, and she probably would have agreed to my proposal, but

I knew someone more suited to her needs. I wrote email introductions between the potential client and my fellow speaker; they met, were thrilled with what each other had to offer, and soon my colleague will be traveling to Ghana to help develop and improve corporate communications in their business community! That put a big smile on my face, my colleague's face, the new client's face, and it'll put smiles on the faces of all those who'll reap the benefits of my colleague's expertise. Talk about a win-win! And speaking of smiling...consider smiling at yourself and smiling at others...often; nine times out of ten, if *you* smile at someone he or she will smile back. Try it. Everyone wins the good feeling of the moment. It costs nothing and is so easy to do.

- **Lighten Your Step:** Put a little spring in your step. Have you ever noticed that one's walk telegraphs one's mood? Be conscious of your upper body carriage. Make sure that your shoulders are stacked in vertical alignment with your hips. You'll stand taller, literally breath easier (because, when you stand tall, you elevate your rib cage so that your lungs have more room for maximum expansion), and instantly feel some rejuvenation! Your body will get the message and, automatically, at least some of a blue mood will fade into the shadows.

- **Let Your Inner Light Out:** Some find daily contemplation or meditation essential for serene functioning in our crazy, topsy-turvy, busy work world. Why not try it? Do it for yourself and for those who must interface with you, day-in and day-out. Literally counting, listing and articulating your workplace blessings can help, too. Try this exercise at the end of your day (perhaps as you travel home, or before drifting off to sleep): "Today, at work I was blessed with....today at work I was also blessed with...and, on top of *this*, today at work I was *extra* blessed with...". You may even see the "blessing" in situations that, at first glance, could only be described as total upsets (seeing the "bless-in-the-mess" of it all). For example: "Today I was blessed with being downsized; now

I'm free to explore other opportunities in my field, or in another direction, altogether, and I probably wouldn't have been willing to do this without a shove!" Having this sort of perspective on such a seemingly disastrous day at work may appear "Pollyanna-ish", but doesn't everyone know at least *one* person who was let go and went on to 'bigger and better" things? It may take a few weeks or months, but they usually end up seeing the downsizing experience as a blessing.

- **Lighten Your Load:** rediscover the "D" word. Or, if you know that you're inclined to be a bit of a control freak, discover the "D" word for the first time. *Delegate!* Do *you* really have to do it all? Give it up, already! Learn that even if some particular piece of work is not completed to your exact standards, maybe "good enough" *is* good enough, in some cases! Learn the strategy of renegotiating deadlines and obligations where need be. Maybe someone else can do some of the work some of the time; and wouldn't it just be the kicker if they ended up being better at it than *you?* Surrender being the office melodrama king or queen who is so crazy busy that they don't even have time to take a washroom break! Know when to say "when" about how much is on your work plate.

- **Lighten Your Language:** There *is* such a thing as "heavy" language. How heavy is your language when going through a blue period? When someone says to you, "How's it going?" Do you respond, "Oh, it's *going*, alright!" When someone says, "Good morning!", do you say, "What's so good about it?" Work hard to lighten your language while pushing through a difficult time. Use positive self-talk, and speak to others, with an upbeat inflection, even if it's a "fake it 'til you make it" proposition.

Redefining Success

> *Life is a succession of moments. To live each one is to succeed.* — Corita Kent

Redefining success is another strategy to help see you through blue periods; it's another way to count your blessings. Ask yourself:

- What does success mean to me?

- What does success mean to the world around me?

- What does success at my job/in my profession mean? in my organization?

- How would I define success in my personal life?

- How does society's prescribed definition of personal and professional success influence my own definition of this concept?

- How can I broaden my personal definition of success?

> *Success is to be measured not so much by the position that one has reached in life as by the obstacles that one has overcome while trying to succeed.*
> — Booker T. Washington

A few years ago I learned a simple yet profound lesson about success from Michael Gelb, who, along with Tony Buzan, co-authored, *Lessons from the Art of Juggling: How to achieve your full potential in business, learning and life.* Mr. Gelb (who, in addition to his academic and business credentials, is also a retired professional juggler) provided each member of his audience with a set of three colourful foam balls and guaranteed we'd *all* be successful in our very first lesson in the art of juggling—which he'd instruct.

How many people do you think actually believed him? Hardly any. But we all got up out of our seats, took our colourful foam balls in hand and played along...and then it happened. We *were* all successful! Every single last one of us! Who knew it could be true? How could that be, you may ask? This is how...Gelb told us that the very first lesson in the art of juggling is the courage to hold all three balls in our hands and then, all at once, throw these three balls into the air and let them all fall to the ground...*on purpose!* Do you think we knew how to do that? You bet! And what a funny sight to see... hundreds of people simultaneously throwing coloured balls into the air, and then watching them cascade to the ground and roll around. It was also pretty funny to see everyone scrambling around on their hands and knees, afterwards, looking to retrieve their balls (by that point no one could really figure out whose were whose)!

The point was this: most people will look at the fallen, lifeless balls on the floor and say "I failed." But maybe these "groundballs" represent *success* after all, because the only way to become a juggler is to have the nerve to grab the balls and give them a throw in the first place! How can you learn to "juggle", at work or elsewhere, if you aren't willing to let go? if you aren't willing to acknowledge the elements of success in a perceived "failure"?

Next time you think you've failed, consider the juggling balls and reconsider your personal definition of success for the particular task. And, when you're *really* in a funk, consider the lifeline lent by the profound words from Clarissa Pinkola Estes (author of *Women Who Run With the Wolves*):

> *There will always be times when you feel discouraged. I too have felt despair many times in my life, but I do not keep a chair for it; I will not entertain it. It is not allowed to eat from my plate. The reason is this: In my uttermost bones I know something, as do you. It is that there can be no despair when you remember why you came to Earth, whom you serve, and who sent you here. The good words we say and the good deeds we do are not ours: They are the words and deeds of the One who brought us here. In that spirit, I hope you will write this on your wall: When a great ship is in harbor and moored, it is safe, there can be no doubt. But that is not what great ships are built for.*

Some will say, "Yeah, yeah...I know all this stuff", while others will roll their eyes at the "New Age-iness" of it all. But there's one thing I've learned through the years that makes for a great rebuttle here: If you *know* it, but you don't *do* it, you *don't* know it, because if you *knew* it, you'd *do* it!

There's a big difference between knowing and believing, but for many the words are interchangeable. Many years ago, a fellow workshop facilitator–the late Jim Quinn–illustrated this point for me with a tongue-in-cheek story and a twinkle in his eye: A man, his wife and seven children, new to town, attend their first Sunday church service. The minister is delighted to welcome nine new parishioners. After the service, he asks the husband, "Are *these* your children?" to which the husband replies, "I believe they are." Next, the minister asks the wife, "Are these *your* children?", to which the wife replies, "I *know* they are"!

Knowing that you're successful, on your own terms, is different than *believing* you are. *Knowing* you'll persevere through difficult times is more assuring than *believing* you will. I recently heard a terrific saying from, of all places, a television drama called *Judging Amy*. One character says to another, "Everything will be fine, in the end. And if it isn't fine...it's not the end!" Another couple of philosophical expressions to help see you or your team through rough times and shore up in-the-moment definitions of professional success include: "That which doesn't kill us makes us stronger", and, "This too shall pass". Use these when you feel the need; they just may do the trick.

Positive attitude and thinking are important foundation stones for realizing both personal and professional success (however you define it), and have everything to do with persevering. Positive attitude and thinking also take a lot of conscious effort and commitment, especially when you can see that your next resting place, coming up just around the bend, is that old familiar "Pity City"...*again.*

Remember in the closing sentences on the chapter on Energy and Enthusiasm I suggested, "it takes 100% of your positive, focused *attitude*, effort and commitment to choose *desserts* over being *stressed*, to successfully work and live in the "new normal"? Well the same applies to the effort required to persevere and succeed at anything...it takes 100% of your commitment—not 99. What good is 99% about anything when the chips are down? Well, to answer that question, playing devil's advocate...if someone told me I had a 99% chance of winning the big lottery, I'd at least go serious window-shopping, even if I didn't actually buy anything outrageously expensive, in advance. If a surgeon told me I had a 99% chance of surviving a serious procedure, I'd probably rest assured that I'd live to see tomorrow. But what happens when, for example, your spouse tells you, "Darling, I'm 99% committed to our relationship"? What goes through your mind when the person to whom you report says, "I'm 99% pleased with your work performance this year"? Most of us would want to know what's going on with the other 1%! As subtle as it may sometimes be, there's definitely an energetic and emotional difference between 100% and 99% of *anything*.

What's the *difference* between 99 and 100% commitment and how does this difference show up in workplace attitudes and behaviours? Can you see and feel the difference between employees who are 100% committed and focused and those who are 99%? between those who give it everything they've got, everyday, and those who always hold some back? and between those who are willing to "soldier on" and persevere despite difficulties versus those who have a "I give up", defeatist attitude? Author/psychologist/therapist Jack Kornfield, in his audio series, *The Inner Art of Meditation*, tells the story of two barnyard animals—a pig and a hen—who break out of their humdrum farm life, travel down a dusty dirt road, full of excitement and wonder as they contemplate the adventures they'll experience. After walking all day and night, they confess to one another just how mighty hungry they feel. No sooner had they acknowledged this truth when, on the horizon, they spotted the glowing red neon sign of a diner. When they arrived at the doorstep, salivating at the thought of a scrumptious breakfast, they paused to read the menu posted outside, "Today's Special: Ham and Eggs". The pig and the hen looked at one another with sinking hearts; they were soooo hungry but, to them, the "special" was out of the question! What should they do? They were so hungry! After a few moments the hen clucked, "Oh what the heck...let's go for it!". To which the pig replied, "NO WAY! For *you* it's just a contribution...for *me* it's 100% commitment!" And *that*, dear reader, is the difference between 99% and 100 % commitment! Perseverance. Commitment. Success. They all hang together.

Getting back, this one last time, to redefining success, consider these words from Ralph Waldo Emerson:

WHAT IS SUCCESS?

To laugh often and love much;

To win the respect of intelligent people

and the affection of children;

To earn the approval of honest critics

and endure the betrayal of false friends;

To appreciate beauty;

To find the best in others;

To give of one's self without the

slightest thought of return;

To have accomplished a task,

whether by a healthy child,

a rescued soul, a garden patch,

or a redeemed social condition;

To have played and laughed with enthusiasm

and sung with exaltation;

To know that even one life has breathed easier because

you have lived;

This is to have succeeded.

– Ralph Waldo Emerson

8

Passion Point #8:
Perpetuate Relationships

Strange is our situation here upon earth. Each of us comes for a short visit, not knowing why, yet sometimes seeming to a divine purpose.

From the standpoint of daily life, however, there is one thing we do know:

That we are here for the sake of others...for the countless unknown souls with whose fate we are connected by a bond of sympathy.

Many times a day, I realize how much my outer and inner life is built upon the labors of people, both living and dead, and how earnestly I must exert myself in order to give in return as much as I have received.

— Albert Einstein

Many years ago, a participant in one of my audiences, as he listened, sketched out illustrations and cartoon situations based on the themes of my presentation. At the end of the day he kindly presented me with his two favourites, one of which pretty much sums up the dog-eat-dog mentality of some workplaces. It shows four men in a rowboat, two in the bow, two in the stern. The boat is rapidly taking on water, and the two men at the rear of the boat are bailing frantically but to no avail. The rowboat is tipped up so that the two men in the bow are high and dry. The bubble caption hangs over the two in the bow, and reads, "We're sure glad the hole isn't at *our* end!"

They don't get it. They don't *get* that if the other end goes down, they do too! They don't *get* that they're, "all in the same boat together"! They aren't, as author Peter Senge (*The Fifth Discipline: The Art & Practice of the Learning Organization*") would say, "Systems Thinking".

Senge popularized the phrase and concept of "systems thinking" for a new generation, but management writers have been contributing to this concept for at least the past 60 years. The oldest volume on this subject in my own personal collection is, coincidentally, entitled *Systems Thinking* (Editor F. E. Emery) and was published in 1969, and that book references research on the subject dating to 1937.

At any rate, in *The Fifth Discipline,* Senge explains the concept of systems thinking. He points out that if a cloud masses, the sky darkens and leaves twist upwards, we know that it will rain. We also know that after the storm, the runoff will feed into the groundwater miles away, and the sky will grow clear by tomorrow. All these events are distant in time and space, and yet they are all part of the same pattern. Each has an influence on the rest, an influence that is usually hidden from view. To understand the rainstorm system, you need to contemplate the whole thing, not just individual parts of the pattern.

Business and other human endeavours are also systems. They, too, are bound by invisible fabrics of interrelated and connected actions that can take years to play out their effect on each other. Since we are part of the whole latticework ourselves, it's hard to see the whole pattern of change. Instead, we tend to focus on snapshots of isolated parts of the system, and wonder why our deepest problems never seem to get solved.

That's exactly what the rowboat picture shows…at least two of these four men are only focusing on a snapshot. And, because of their shortsightedness, *all* the sailors may be destined to go down, down, down! Each member of that boat could easily represent members of one work team. Alternatively, each man could represent a work team within a division, or four divisions at one location, or four different regional offices, or four companies in the same field. Are they all in the boat together or not? When it comes to your own team or workplace...are you all in *your* boat...together? Do you ever find yourself gloating that the "hole" isn't at your end?

When we work hard to grow and nurture positive, productive workplace relationships, we care more about what happens to and with the "other guy". The caring may spring from a growing sense of *agape* (selfless love or affection) towards our colleagues, or from a better understanding of the larger system at work; that what happens to *others* will also (immediately or eventually) happen to *us*. Regardless, committing to building positive relationships with colleagues and clients helps everyone reach their goals. Getting connected (or reconnected), and *staying* connected with those in your workplace circle of influence helps everyone bail out of "leaky" situations.

You're More Connected Than You Think

Call it a clan, call it a network, call it a tribe, call it a family. Whatever you call it, whoever you are, you need one. — Jane Howard

Nurturing and growing relationships is about recognizing relationship possibilities that are right under your nose, and fledgling relationships in which promise and potential exist. Everyone is more connected than they may first realize. I've heard it said that every person knows an average of 250 people. Imagine—if *you* know 250 people, and each of they know 250 people, you start to see how the concept of "six degrees of separation" may be true.

Everyone has at least a tale or two that shows what a small world it is that we live in. During another of my visits to England, we lunched in a grand old inn in Richmond, where our server asked if I was American. "No...an honest mistake...I'm Canadian", I replied. She told me her chef was from Canada, and later brought her out to meet us.

I asked the cook where she was from, and, like me, she was

from Toronto. I asked her what neighbourhood she lived in, to which she replied, "The Annex". Well, so did I. It turned out that we lived on the same street ten doors away from one another for the past ten years and never knew each other! What are the odds? Some might say the odds are pretty good when you consider the stereotypical anonymity of a big city; never-the-less, I went all the way to England, to a little town up the Thames River, only to discover a neighbour cooking my lunch!

We wouldn't have even know this if we'd not acted and followed up on small-talk, curiosities, self-disclosed and listened for more information. Everyone *does* have at least a tale or two to illustrate what a small world it is—what're yours? You really *are* more connected than you think. Remember this especially when you feel alone, and think you don't know anyone who can help you out.

Here's another of my personal small world stories, with a more decidedly, in the end, networking twist: after delivering a keynote for a new client's conference a few years ago, I drove home a dipsy-doodle way I hadn't taken in 20 years (thanks to my intimate knowledge of west-end back streets of Toronto and late afternoon grid-locked traffic). Nostalgia welled up in me as I went by my old high school, and then, my heart sank. Mr. Alexander, a best-loved phys. ed. teacher, had passed away and the farewell was posted outside the school. I hadn't thought of him since 1976. I'll share more on what the news of this teacher's passing inspired for me later in this chapter, but first, let me digress...back to the conference at which I'd just spoken.

Before I began my keynote address at that conference, a woman approached me and said, "We know each other!" I agreed but it took moments before we realized the connection was a running clinic we'd both attended earlier that year. We were delighted at the coincidence. Then, still before I started my keynote, *another* person approached and said, "Do you remember me? Last year you facilitated a management workshop I attended at my previous employer's place!" Wow! What are the odds of that happening? I'm beginning to realize they're greater than we think. I was even once approached at a funeral home, while paying respects! The older you get, and the more you're out there, the more it's bound to happen. The question is, are you going to remember those from your past—and, even more, are *they* going to remember *you*—fondly and with enthusiasm, or cynically and with contempt? Are those others, with whom you've previously connected, going to go out of their way to say hello or are they going to do their level best to avoid you at all costs? You have quite a bit of influence over that two-sided choice of others.

If you're looking for amazing and provocative tips, techniques and strategies for being remembered fondly, I highly encourage you to read, *Dig Your Well Before You're Thirsty: The Only Networking Book You'll Ever Need*, by Harvey Mackay. *The Seven Habits of Highly Effective People* author, Stephen Covey's, testimonial for *Dig Your Well* reads: A mother lode of timely, hard-earend, bite-size, street-smart golden nuggets...invaluable for job seekers, employed or unemployed." Couldn't say it better, myself!

There have been volumes written on effective strategies for networking and sincerely and authentically connecting with others. Harvey Mackay, and another quintessential champion of quality networking, author and motivational speaker, Zig Zigglar, are experts at encouraging their readers and audiences to examine and reflect on how well they're connecting with people that are important to them.

How well are *you* networking with people that are important in your life? Zig Ziggler espouses the idea that the way to help yourself get what *you* want is to help other people get what *they* want...and to do so with a sincere and open heart. This same philosophy was captured in the movie *First Knight*, in which Sean Connery played King Arthur and Richard Gere played Sir Lancelot. When King Arthur introduced Sir Lancelot to the Round Table, he pointed out the inscription carved in the table, "Through service to others, we serve ourselves". When I saw that, I thought, "Wow! The original team builder! The original networker!"

Knowing how to network—how to ask for help and how to give it—is a survival skill in today's workplace.
— Janis Foord Kirk

Networking means connecting, staying connected and/or reconnecting with people you admire, respect and value...and it's just as valuable and important for colleagues *within* an organization to network with each other, as it is for entrepreneurs and the self-employed.

Here are five suggestions for elevating your networking effectiveness:

1. **Work hard on a sincere and friendly tone of voice, especially on the phone.** As I first suggested in Chapter One, practice by changing your voice mail daily; decide—before recording your greeting—how you'd like to come across to incoming callers. Then, before you save the greeting, *play it back and listen to it* to make sure it sounds the way you want. If it doesn't...rub it out and start again, even if it takes a half-dozen tries. With practice, you'll get it right first time almost every time out. When you're not available, your message represents you. Ask yourself: Is my greeting representing me well, or does it make people hang up without leaving a message? If you can't assess this for yourself, ask someone whose opinion you respect to listen to your greeting and give you his or her impression. By the way...you'll know you've got it right when you start getting complimentary messages from callers who say they want to call you every day, just to hear your message and get a lift! Once you get *that* level of welcoming tone in your recorded greeting, I guarantee you'll receive this kind of feedback. Try it! People want to stay in touch with you even more if they consider you a source of inspiration. It makes them *want* to do business with you. It makes them proud to recommend you to others.

2. **Ask lots of questions, in friendly conversation, of people you meet.** Practice with neighbours over the backyard fence, with the person seated next to you on a flight and with colleagues, too. When you hear a point of concern or interest, if you have the resources and connections, help point the way ahead by offering to connect people with others you know (refer to point #3 for more suggestions about this). Work hard at increasing your own comfort with sharing information.

3. **Always, always, always ask permission** of your friend, acquaintance, colleague or family member *before* referring a third person to your contact. Being the conduit for introductions shows good grace and etiquette.

4. **Say thank-you, often and in a diversity of ways.** After I've helped connect two good people, I love the boost of getting a call or email that says, "Thanks...I appreciated your help!" Most of us like to know when we've helped others get what they want. If someone helps *you*, be sure to thank the individual for the part he/she played in *you* getting what you wanted. If you get to the point where you call them multiple times with your thanks for many different kindnesses, boy, will they "get it" that they're making a contribution! Let's face it, sometimes we slug away, day-by-day, doing what we know is good work, without the kudos or reinforcement that indicate that we make a difference. Make sure you let people know they've made a difference for you.

5. **Do What You Love: The Money Will Follow,** so says the book of that title by Marsha Sinetar. It's the same with networking. Sincerely love to network and the opportunities will naturally follow. Trust the process and see for yourself.

Knowledgeable people know facts. Successful and prosperous people know people. — John Demartini

It's easier to keep your focus and passion for your profession in uncertain times (or any time, for that matter), if you interact with energetic and enthusiastic people inside your organization. Especially if those people do the same work as you, or clearly understand your role. But what if there aren't any (or perhaps too few) such colleagues? What if you feel all alone at times? What else can you do?

Ask yourself these questions (and also consider asking your staff to respond, even if it's only in an introspective way, and not for general discussion):

1. **With whom, at work, do I enthusiastically talk shop?** (Not belly-

ache, whine or complain to, but honestly talk and share ideas.) Remember, enthusiasm is contagious and misery loves company, as the old sayings go. So what's it going to be...enthusiastically sharing with upbeat coworkers or taking the "'woe is me" route? Which will keep you happier and living longer?

2. **With whom do I enthusiastically talk shop or exchange professional ideas outside my workplace?** This is important to help you grow some lateral perspective about your work.

3. **How can I expand my network of people who share my professional interests?** Often, people choose the same predictable ways to connect with people and miss out on others. You could join a professional association or another group that interests you; attend publicly sponsored professional conferences; attend events hosted and championed by your employer...to meet others from your workplace whose paths do not usually cross your own, or volunteer for a cause which is near and dear to your heart.

4. **With whom do I share professional victories?** Everyone can use a safe co-worker with whom they can tell their frustrations when the going gets rough. Let's face it: sometimes it's tiring explaining the politics, intricacies and quirks of all the workplace players to family or friends. The very thought of spending twenty minutes explaining the background before even getting to the story is enough to make you stop talking about work altogether. When you need to get something off your chest—or to share your victories—your trusted workplace buddies are sometimes the best people to go to.

5. **How big and diverse is my network?** Start brainstorming your list of 250 people. Is it easy or hard to get going? Do you notice that you are top heavy with some sorts of people and lacking in others?

Ask yourself, "Whom do I know, who knows me back, in the following fields:

- Professional associations (in my own province or state, and beyond)

- Organizational/professional development (in my own organization and beyond)

- Human resources

- Association administration, executives and/or board members

- Information technology

- Education, teaching, post-secondary education, university, community college

- Real estate

- Financial institutions, banking, credit unions, investment houses

- Executive search/headhunters

- Travel, tourism, hospitality

- Politics, local or otherwise

- Law

- Entertainment, film, music, theatre, celebrity

- Insurance

- Media, TV, radio, publishing, newspapers, magazine

- Sales and marketing, communications, promotions, public relations

- Medicine, hospital administration

- Veterinarian

- Religious community(s)

- Law enforcement/police

- Firefighting

- and any other category you think should also be on this list!

Observe the gaps and work on a strategy for ensuring that you know at least one authentic contact in a wide diversity of fields that matter to you most.

6. **Do I want to grow my network of internal and external profession-al connections?** If "yes", move on to number 7. If "no"...you're all done.

7. **Today, tomorrow, next week and next month, what am I willing to do to make that happen?** "A journey of thousand miles begins with that first step", says the ancient Chinese proverb, so decide what *one* thing you will do immediately, and then later on, to expand your circle of relations and influence.

Always remember the power of *your* primary 250-person circle of influence. Get out there; strangers are only friends you've yet to meet! Make their acquaintance *now*, so that you may *honestly* consider them part of your network, *before* you need their help. Have you ever been really sloppy about staying in touch with people you genuinely like, admire or need to have on your side, using the tired excuse of being too crazy busy to call? Then one day you contact someone out of the blue for a favour, and feel like a schmuck because you only ever call when you need something? *You* know you're being a "taker"—and *they* know it, too!

Do what you can, in creative and time-efficient ways, to stay in touch with those who matter. Here's why...almost every-one now has call display! If you only ever connect with another when you *need* something...guess what? That coveted person on the other end of the line may just decide to let your call go to voice mail. To paraphrase Marianne Williamson (author of *A Return to Love, Illuminata, A Woman's Worth* and others), if you have friends and colleagues who believe in you, trust you and honour you as a person of integrity and ethics, and you lose all your money...someone can give you a loan, but *no one* can loan you the power to have your calls returned. It's the law of the harvest—you reap what you sow.

And that brings me back to the beloved high school teacher who passed away...the one I mentioned near the start of this chapter...the one whose passing I learned of while driving by my old high school, returning from a local speaking engagement. That sad news made me realize that there have been a few really important teachers in my life (I hope it's the same for you, too). I got to thinking that they probably didn't know how very special they were and what valuable contributions they made. Many think about tracking down favourite teachers but few actually do it. All of a sudden it became urgently important to me to find and talk with Mr. McCullough, my Grade 10 geography teacher, and Miss Lakatos, my Grade 6 teacher. I contacted my old schools. The administrative assistants at both schools said they'd somehow get messages to these teachers. Within two hours both responded! I had a wonderful luncheon with Mr. McCullough and finally got to tell him what an inspiration he'd been. His teaching style and firm but kind insistence that there was more in me than I was giving was the beginning of my academic success.

I also had the most lovely and heartfelt conversation with my Grade 6 teacher, who had demonstrated a fun-loving and respectful teaching style that made me feel like an adult, and I flourished under her tutelage. We, too, decided to meet for lunch, and the rest is history. You know, she's only ten years my senior (no wonder she was so "hip" and "groovy" back in 1969...she was only 21!). Today, these few years later, my Miss Lakatos (Gladman), a.k.a. "Judy", is one of my dearest friends. Who'd have thunk? My private life is enriched for having drawn Judy into my circle. That's reward enough for me. The serendipitous bonus is that Judy has a powerful circle of influence of her own and has been a wonderful champion of my work and services.

Let the magic of networking, nurturing and growing relationships work for you, whether it's at a job and a company you've been with for 20 years, or whether you're between professional opportunities. Act on whimsical ideas. Let them out of the box! Use your intuition. All you really need is a little trust and faith.

Here's my assignment for you:

Ask yourself, "With whom would I reconnect if I only had the time and the nerve?"

Now ask yourself, "What's stopping me?"

Finding *your* "lost" people is probably easier than you think. At the end of the day, all of business (and life, too, for that matter), is not about work...it's about people and relationships and connections.

Like It or Not...Likeability Counts!

I told my psychiatrist that everyone hates me. He said I was being ridiculous—everyone hasn't met me yet.
— Rodney Dangerfield

How likeable are *you*? What evidence can you cite to confirm your response to this question? Do you possibly suffer from "Dangerfielditis"? Or, how about that old Girl Guides and Scouts song, "Nobody likes me, everybody hates me, I'm going to the garden to eat worms...(yum yum)"? Recall the Chapter One quote from George Bernard Shaw, "In the right key anything can be said. In the wrong key, nothing." Think of the charmed people *you* know who can get away with comments that are eyebrow rising or provocative, with a twinkle in their eye and a curl on their lips, while others remain smiling and affectionately engaged. There's one in every workplace and in every family and in every group of friends. You've probably just said their name silently or even aloud! How *do* they get away with it? A high likeability factor is probably the answer.

Likeability makes the difference in how you're received and how your message and direction are embraced, and often it matters *not* what your positional status is in the organization.

To some extent, projecting likeability can't be taught. It has to be learned and demonstrated by the heart, from the inside out. However, there are ways to increase rapport and trust with those whom you interact that raise your likeability rating.

Here are 12 suggestions for becoming more likeable:

1. **Remember people's names and use them in conversation.** Don't let yourself off the hook with that tired old excuse, "I'm ter-

rible with names"; figure out a way to get better at it. Make a game of it, if you must. Use rhymes (in your head, of course), or some other triggering link—do they have the same name as someone else you know, or someone famous that you'll remember?

2. If you find yourself giving a formal presentation, and someone from the audience asks you a question, **echo back that person's exact words and use the metaphors they used to illustrate their points.** People understand and relate to your answers best if you echo their words.

3. **Thank people sincerely and in various ways.** It only takes three minutes to write a thank-you card with three or four sentences in it (and even less if you prefer email). Can you find one extra set of three minutes a day to write *one* thank-you note, or even leave a voice mail of appreciation? I bet you can.

4. **Smile.** I've noticed that most people don't walk around with a smile on their face, but if *I* smile first, nine times out of ten, *they* smile back! I think I first started experimenting with this when I was still in high school and came across this passage:

> *A smile costs nothing, but it creates much.*
>
> *It enriches those who receive it without impoverishing those who give it. It happens in a flash, and the memory of it may last forever. None are so rich that they can get along without it, and none so poor that they cannot be richer for its benefits. It creates happiness in the home, fosters goodwill in business and is the countersign of friendship.*
>
> *It is rest to the weary, daylight to the discouraged, sunshine to the sad, and is nature's best antidote for trouble. Yet it cannot be begged, bought, borrowed or stolen, for it is something that is worth nothing to any-*

one until it is given away. In the course of the day, some
of your acquaintances (and I'll add "colleagues, clients
or customers, too") may be too tired to give you a
smile. Give them one of yours. Nobody needs a smile
so much as those who have none left to give.

— Anonymous

5. **Don't just look at colleagues, clients, friends and family...see them!** When you meet someone new, make sure you look long enough to note the colour of the person's eyes. You may be surprised to discover how many spouses don't know the colour of their partner's eyes! Much of the time we look at each other, in professional and in personal situations, without truly *seeing* each other. When you sincerely look at and see another, there is an automatic twinkle in your eye that adds to your sincere charisma and likeability.

6. **When dealing with a difficult or closed colleague or client, maintain your kind and warm professionalism at all times.** Try thinking the following as you deal with said difficult person: "I respect you and I acknowledge you even if I don't understand you." Reminding yourself of this, *and sincerely believing it*, will usually cause the other to intuitively realize that you're open to them, no matter what. This strategy may work wonders in a heated debate over a delicate issue during a strained workplace meeting.

7. **When in a conversation, observe the other's body language and subtly mirror it back.** Sometimes we don't know why we instantly like a particular person, but when it comes down to it, it's often because they move and talk as we do. That feels safe and comfortable and so we open up. If you want the other person to be more open, make sure that you're consciously aware of the body language you transmit; uncross your arms, examine your body orientation compared to theirs. Are you shoulder-to-shoulder during your conversation or squarely face-to-face? Your choice of body orientation may vary depending with whom you're speaking (a friend, a client, your biggest "boss", a man or a

woman). According to author Dr. Pat Heim, in her video, *Invisible Rules: Men, Women and Teams*, and also in her book (with Susan Golant), *Hardball for Women: Winning at the game of business*, when communicating in a gregarious fashion men have a strong preference for speaking with others in a shoulder-to-shoulder style, while women prefer to be square on. This works fine when speaking with one's own gender but gets a little tricky when one gender is addressing another. Dr. Heim says that whether we realize it or not, often-times when speaking with the opposite sex one or both of the parties are trying to get the communicating body orientation "fixed up", eg. a woman may consciously or unconsciously feel that a *shoulder-to-shoulder* chat at the workplace water cooler with a male counterpart is too cool, impersonal or unfriendly, and so shuffles her feet to talk with the man *squarely*. In subconscious "male culture", a standing, square-on conversation with another male is usually reserved for disagreement or confrontation (which is why you so often see this scenario on the cover of sports magazines—coaches squarely facing referees, yelling their heads off at each other!). Do you get this dynamic? The woman shuffles *her* feet to get square with the man with whom she's speaking; and then, in response to the discomfort of the square orientation, the man shuffles *his* feet to re-establish the more comfortable shoulder-to-shoulder/"buddy" body orientation. Both parties end up going around in literal circles trying to get things "fixed up"! Dr. Heim's suggestion for curing this body orientation dilemma is "stay planted", regardless of your gender. Understand and be aware of the subtle communicative challenges around body language; make it easier for the other guy by standing still and letting him or her establish the body orientation that will exist between the two of you while you talk. For another incredibly well-researched, insightful and even funny look at the topic and challenge of communication between the sexes, I also highly recommend that you read authors Barbara and Allan Pease's book, *Why Men Don't Listen and Women Can't Read Maps: How we're different and what to do about it.*

8. **Consciously observe others' preferred learning style…**is it auditory, visual or hands on? People's word choices will help you figure this one out, eg. "I *hear* you", "I *see* what you mean", "*Describe* how it works". Once identified, mirror back the learning style that the other has unconsciously telegraphed to you. Delivering your message in the other's preferred style helps get your point across.

9. **Practice your voice inflection.** Remember my earlier reference, in Chapter One, to that old saying, "It's not what you say, it's how you say it?" There may be more times than you've ever imagined when you've used a tone of voice that has either mildly or seriously offended another. Agree? Practice conscious tone of voice daily.

10. **Be a chameleon when communicating by voicemail or email.** Some people like a little small talk before getting down to business; others stay on task and immediately get to the point. When the other starts the communication cycle using their own style (provided it's professionally acceptable enough, even if it's not quite your style), or when you're especially desirous of building a relationship with that individual, communicate the way they do. Sometimes this will go against your grain, but if you can stomach it, it will help the other person relate to you.

11. **Self-Disclose.** Share personal anecdotes that relate to the point you're addressing. They make you seem more three-dimensional. It makes others laugh, and when we laugh together, a relationship grows.

12. **Pay attention to the disclosures your colleagues and clients share (make either clear mental or literal notes to help your recollection).** For example, I learned that one of my clients had a sick puppy and didn't have a vet because she was new to Toronto. I recommended mine. Her puppy recovered, and now, every once in a while we bump into each other at the vet's! Another was on the brink of becoming a grandparent for the 20th time (that seemed pretty remarkable to me), and yet another turned out to be my brother-in-law's brother!

Practicing building rapport and likeability goes a long way to doing your job well and helps you through all kinds of unexpected situations. Developing rapport and likeability with colleagues and clients isn't necessarily a natural gift—it's often a learned skill that, as a professional, you *can* master. It's not what you get from it...it's how much further you can go, or how much more effective the two of you can be together, because of it. Rapport and likeability are the prerequisites for establishing trust. Once others trust you—as their guide, manager, friend, mentor or whatever—the heavens open. And *that's* the big win for everyone concerned!

The Art of Giving and Receiving Feedback as Yet Another Way to Grow and Nurture Relationships

O' wad some poower the giftie gi'e us, tae see o'orsels as ithers see us. — Rabbie Burns

I've always found this passage by this beloved Scottish poet to be profoundly true. Thanks to my dear Scottish friend, Helen Wilkie, I'm able to provide you the authentic Scottish version of this passage and the following translation, which may be a bit clearer: "Oh would some, the gift give us, to see ourselves as others see us." Or, "Would someone please give us the gift of seeing ourselves as others see us". We'd all benefit tremendously from heeding at least some of the feedback of others.

Remember the schoolyard bully who wielded power over all the kids? Was there one in your school who bragged, "If I have something to say about you, I'll tell it to your face?" Now we meet those same bullies, all grown up, in our communities and workplaces. At work, there's a good chance that some have made it to middle management and beyond. These one-time schoolyard bullies may not present the same way they did when they were 11 or 12 years old (at least not on the surface), but it's amazing how character traits established by Grade 6 manifest in today's workplace.

I once attended a team meeting where the chairperson strongly and rudely articulated his opinion about a team member's "quirks and preferences." It was an over-the-top explosion, shocking all in the room, including the person to whom the words were directed. The chair then said, as if sensing the need to defend his outburst, "Hey, we're all adults here! I'm just calling a spade a spade. I'm calling it the way I see it. I'm speaking the truth here!" A lot of damage was done to that team's harmony and synergy in just a few moments...all in the name of the "truth".

Many employees have had the good fortune of exposure to professional development and training on effective communication skills. Many take these opportunities to heart and commit to being lifelong students of these practices. Yet we *still* witness colleagues, whom we thought knew better, being grossly inappropriate in their conversations, hiding behind the cloak of, "We're all adults here...we all understand the importance of giving feedback, so I'm letting it rip!" It's even worse when those "communicators" are in leadership positions. I've often heard my workshop participants say that those who *most* need to attend workshops on leadership and communication *never* attend; or if they do attend, it's once or twice, with arrogance and a, "Just *try* to teach me something. I dare you.", attitude.

A little information is a dangerous thing.
— Anonymous

I subscribe to the old adage of a little information being a dangerous thing. Too often people apply effective communication concepts out of context. Some say they embrace higher-level thinking about how and when to give feedback, and then thoughtlessly pop off personal thoughts masquerading as "feedback", without reflecting why the words are jumping out of their mouths in the first place.

There's a feedback tyranny happening in some organizations and it's damaging workplace relationships. Many people are of the opinion that if they feel an urge to give someone feedback, they have the right, obligation and organizational duty to do so the split second it occurs to them.

Some parents tell their children, "If you can't say anything nice, don't say anything at all." Did yours? In business, this isn't always the best way to move ahead, so if you wish to declare yourself, and be perceived by others, as a masterful communicator (or at least dutiful student of the subject), remember that there are good ways and bad ways to deliver feedback.

If you sincerely wish to grow and nurture workplace relationships, here are some suggestions to consider before going ahead and giving feedback:

- **Develop your introspective skills;** ask yourself, "What are my motives for wanting to give this feedback?" Be sure there's a real problem or issue that won't go away if it's not addressed. Could it be that you're just in a bad mood?

- **Identify the real issue(s),** not just the symptoms, presenting issue(s) or personalities; realize there's often something beyond the issue that triggers the knee-jerk desire to give feedback

- **Be prepared to work towards a mutually agreeable solution** rather than *winning*; think "*solution*-oriented" rather than "*problem* solving" (this is the old positive thinking focus coming to the fore once again)

- **Remember that it's alright to disagree;** the other person is not "bad" if he or she disagrees with you

- **Keep your perspective;** rather than destroying a relationship, choosing to work towards a mutually satisfying solution can enhance it

While working on an issue remember to:

- **Ask yourself whether you experience the issue as a preference or a value.** Are you willing to let go of at least some preferences and, instead, reserve feedback for issues related to your values? I first addressed this comparison of "preferences" versus "values" in Chapter Three, where I suggested that *values* are worth sticking up and fighting for, as they're bone deep personal beliefs anchored in family or culture traditions with which we still actively, passionately and consciously agree. *Preferences,* on the other hand, usually muster up much less "fire in the belly"; we may *prefer* something to be this way or that, but we know that we can live with another way, if we must...if we don't "get our own way" on a particular issue. If we must surrender a *preference,* we usually don't loose much sleep over it, but we just might over a *value. Preferences* (at least some of them) could be surrendered...for the sake of maintaining ongoing professional relationships and for your own sanity

- **Look for classic "win-win" solutions**—although, through the eyes of the cynic, looking for the "win-win" is just way too "new age-ie", win-wins *are* out there...they *do* exist and often times can be achieved, if you care to work at it

- **Empathize with the other's perspective;** put yourself in their shoes

- **Acknowledge to yourself and to the other person that part of the problem that belongs to you;** to ensure your sincerity in owning up to your part, be sure that you can specifically identify what part *is* your fault, and why

- *Talk* **about your feelings instead of acting on them**

- **Establish a common goal and stay focused on it**

- **Be persistent** in coming to a satisfactory solution if the issue is important to you

- **At the end of the discussion with the other, summarize what's been decided,** who will take any next steps and set a follow-up date for checking in with one another to see how things are going

Remember, feedback is most helpful if it's:

- **Descriptive, not evaluative:** "You interrupted him twice," rather than, "You're not a good listener."

- **Specific versus general:** "I like the way you praised Peter for handling that situation," rather than, "You always give good emotional support to your staff."

- **Solicited versus imposed:** When we impose feedback, the other person may feel defensive; when feedback is solicited, there's a better chance your feedback will be well received

- **Well-timed:** Offer feedback soon after the event related to the situation you're discussing (provided that you believe the receiver is ready and willing to hear your thoughts)

- **Focused on modifiable behaviour:** frustration is only increased when people are reminded of shortcomings over which they feel they have no control. Offer feedback on attitudes and behaviours you *know* the receiver has the ability and openness to modify, if he or she cares to listen and make the effort to adjust

- **Considerate of the needs of the receiver and giver:** offer feedback from a position of caring, sincerely expressed. People can tell when so called "caring words", supposedly offered in their "best interest", aren't heartfelt; pay attention to the needs of the person on the receiving end of the feedback

- **Validated with the receiver:** before you offer feedback, get the receiver's perspective on the topic; after giving the feedback, check that the information you offered was heard and accurately received, and be quick—get your point across and seek the reciever's response *within 60 seconds,*otherwise the receiver may feel attacked and become defensive; be succinct with your opening comments

- **Not a demand for change:** we often give feedback as a way of demanding that someone change; when feedback is sincerely and consciously offered, it's not a demand for change, it's simply a sharing of information, which the receiver can then apply as he or she chooses

Once again, above all, remember George Bernard Shaw's words when you're giving feedback, "In the right key, anything can be said, in the wrong key, nothing. The only delicate part is the establishment of the key!"

You could keep busy becoming masterful at giving and receiving feedback all the rest of your days. There will be times when you'll forget, or choose not to use your feedback skills. Sometimes you might kick yourself afterwards for succumbing to an emotional reaction; you knew better and blurted something regretful, anyway. Cut yourself some slack when those moments occur. Everyone periodically falls off the wagon. When you do, celebrate that at least you now have the awareness to assess what you did "wrong", and know how to improve next time.

So back to, *"O' wad some poower the giftie gi'e us, tae see o'orsels as ithers see us."* As an aside, for your hidden Scot within, I have it on good authority that one must always refer to Robert Burns as "Rabbie" and never "Robbie". So there you go...apply this savvy, inside Scottish wisdom on Rabbie Burns Day next January 25th!

Listening to Others With Heart

> *Listen to everyone in your company, and figure out ways to get them talking. The folks on the front line — the ones who actually talk to customers — are the only ones who really know what's going on out there. You'd better find out what they know.*
> — Sam Walton

Growing and nurturing your workplace relationships is about active listening as much as it's about acting, networking and speaking. "You can listen as well as you hear", so says the song "The Living Years", by the 1980's group *Mike and The Mechanics*. But can we? Do we...day-in and day-out? Can most of us do better, when it comes to honest-to-goodness listening? How about yourself? Do you see the links between your personal sense of leadership, your ability to demonstrate effective listening and getting more of the results you desire and expect?

Leadership authority Warren Bennis states, "The basis of

leadership is the capacity of the leader to change the mindset, the framework, of another person." In other words, leaders move people towards common goals by helping them see the world differently. One of the subtle and magical ways to help facilitate *that* in others is to listen really hard to what they have to say.

Some employees "follow the leader" out of fear, however, the most effective leaders gain employees' devotion by being motivational, informed, dependable, visionary, inspiring and, yes, even by being charismatic and interesting people (and you'll probably find that these leaders got that way by being fine listeners).

How do you get others to care enough to take the time to bother telling you something you may really need to know? Listen. Show sincere and patient interest in what they have to say and watch what happens next.

Steven B. Sample, the 10th president of the University of Southern California, in the Autumn, 2000 edition of USC Trojan Family Magazine: *The Art and Adventure of Collaborating with Warren Bennis*, shared:

> *One of Warren Bennis' axioms is that a leader should be able to bring out the best in those around him. In making that case, Warren loves to cite an old story about the difference between 19th-century British Prime Ministers William Gladstone and Benjamin Disraeli. It was said that, when you had dinner with Gladstone, you left feeling he was the wittiest, most brilliant, most charming person on earth. But when you had dinner with Disraeli, you left feeling that you were the wittiest, most brilliant, charming person on earth. In this respect, Bennis and Disraeli are exactly alike. Warren's magnificently fine-tuned personal radar makes him extremely sensitive and receptive to what other people are thinking, feeling and saying. I've never encountered a person who is a better listener who has that rare ability to make you feel as though you were the only person in the world.*

In a nutshell...to be interesting, be interested.

One of the trickiest challenges you can give yourself is to have a conversation without once using the word "I". Try it, and see how challenging it can be. Remember that old expression, "there's no 'I' in team work"? Once we start into "I..." this, and "I..." that, we're not listening.

Most everyone is periodically guilty of not listening, and there are all sorts of manifestations of this failure in interpersonal communications in the workplace by both leaders and others.

Look over these Classic Examples of Poor Listening Habits (originally outlined in A Handbook of Structured Experiences for Human Relations Training, published by University Associates Publishers); even if only to yourself, admit when you must confess, "I do that one; I do that one; and, oh brother, I do that one, too!":

1. **Not paying attention:** Listeners may allow themselves to be distracted or to think of something else. Not *wanting* to listen also contributes to lack of attention.

2. **Pseudo-listening:** Often, people who are thinking about something else deliberately try to look as though they're listening. Such pretence may leave the speaker with the impression that the listener has heard their important information or instructions.

3. **Listening but not hearing:** Sometimes a person listens only to facts or details or to the way they were presented and misses the real meaning.

4. **Rehearsing:** Some people listen until they want to say something; then they stop listening, start rehearsing what they have to say, and wait for the opportunity to jump in and talk.

5. **Interpreting:** The listener does not wait until the complete meaning can be determined, but interrupts so forcefully that the speaker stops in mid-sentence.

6. **Hearing what is expected:** People frequently hear what they expect the other to say; alternatively, they refuse to hear what they don't want to hear.

7. **Feeling defensive:** The listener assumes he or she knows the speaker's intention for saying something, and for whatever reason, expects to be attacked.

8. **Listening for a point of disagreement:** Some listeners seem to wait for the chance to attack someone. They listen intently for points on which they can disagree and then attack or confront.

Anyone can learn better listening habits if they choose to turn off the autopilot and adopt some new practices.

> *Listening, not imitation, may be the sincerest form of flattery.* — Dr. Joyce Brothers

Here are a few suggestions that can help you become a better listener:

1. **Pay attention:** Force yourself to pay attention to the speaker. If you find the speaker dull, use extra effort to stay focused on his or her words and feelings. Use nonverbal cues (such as eye contact, head nods, and smiles) to acknowledge that you're *sincerely* listening.

2. **Listen for the whole message:** Look for meaning and consistency, or congruence, in both the speaker's verbal and nonverbal messages, and listen for ideas, feelings, intentions and facts. Be open, honest and vigilant about your possible prejudices, so that you'll accurately hear what you may otherwise find unpleasant or unwelcome.

3. **Hear before evaluating:** Listen without drawing a premature conclusion; suspend judgment while the other is talking. By questioning the speaker in a non-accusing/sincerely inquisitive manner, rather than giving advice or opinion, you can often discover exactly what the speaker has in mind.

4. **Paraphrase what you heard:** Non-judgmentally paraphrasing the speaker's words, and asking if that is what was meant, goes a long way to keeping your interpretations correct. If you're uncertain about the meaning or intent behind the

speaker's words, put the onus on yourself to clarify, rather than waiting and hoping that the speaker will do so.

5. **Ask if there's anything else you should know:** Sometimes we hope the answer to such a question is, "No!". Realize that when someone is opening up and telling you valuable details and information, you might as well hear it all in one shot!

> *Listening is a magnetic and strange thing, a creative force. The friends who listen to us are the ones we move toward, and we want to sit in their radius (and this goes for customers, colleagues and clients, too).*
>
> *When we are listened to, it creates us, makes us unfold and expand. I discovered this a few years ago. Before that, when I went to a party I would think anxiously: Now try hard, be lively. But now I tell myself to listen with affection to anyone who talks to me. This person is showing me his soul. It is a little dry and meager and full of grinding talk just now, but soon he will begin to think. He will show his true self, will be wonderfully alive.*
>
> — Dr. Karl Menninger

Poor listening habits can evolve and crystallize early in life and continue throughout, especially if they're never brought to one's attention. Whole families can be poor listeners and, if you know what I'm talking about from personal experience, you'll know that it's absolutely amazing to observe such a brood when they get together for high holidays or other annual family festivities. It can be truly mind-boggling! The same goes for whole teams and even whole organizations.

When you identify gaps in your listening habits, you can begin to change them. When practicing new approaches, start with those you know best. This very week, take the time to show those of whom you are most fond (at work and home) how much you care. How about showing them with a bit of heightened listening? Practicing your new dedication to active listening with your loved ones, first, is safe. Later, you can take your honed listening skills to work, to show cherished colleagues and clients how much you care about *them*, and what they have to say, too! Listen, as yet another valuable strategy for getting passion out of your profession.

It's all right to hold a conversation as long as you let go of it once in a while. — Anonymous

Nature arranges it so that we can't shut our ears but that we can shut our mouths. — Anonymous

9

Putting it All Together...Class Starts Now!

This is not the end, it is not even the beginning of the end. But it is, perhaps, the end of the beginning.
— Winston Churchill

Whether attending a one-day professional development workshop or a semester-long course, we often think that class starts on the first day of the instructional event and finishes when that event concludes. In fact, the classroom experience is merely an introduction to the *real* class...the class of life. It's only when you get out of the classroom—out of the theory of instruction and suggestion—that you can apply what you've learned. Only *then* can you master your new skills and take them onto the wide-open road of life and amaze yourself, and perhaps others, too, with what you've absorbed along the way.

Here endeth the prelude to "Getting Passion Out of Your Profession". It's time to decide to keep on loving your living, come what may...and you just know there'll be plenty. Class starts now!
— Nina Spencer

Remember to find ways each and every day to:

1. **Practice Positive Thinking and Word Choice:** Consciously choose positive language and thinking to influence your passion for your work, and to inspire the passion of others.

2. **Project Professional Self-Worth:** To really get a hit of the fine contribution you make, be willing to acknowledge, to yourself and others, how well you do what you do!

3. **Protect Sense of Humour:** Laughter is good for your health *and* spirit. Guard against diseases like Psychosclerosis (hardening of the thinking) and HDS (Humour Deficiency Syndrome), which slip into workplace settings and zap everyone's passion. Be the one who starts the humour cycle instead of the anger cycle.

4. **Play with Perspective:** Perspective has everything to do with how you think about control. What do you control? What don't you control? Who do you control? Who don't you control? Think of control like the weather; when you go outside you get whatever's there! It's up to *you* to modify your perspective, so that you can deal with the workplace weather.

5. **Profess Your Purpose:** It's easier to stay the course when you know why you're doing what you're doing. Having a clear, larger purpose helps. Try the five "whys" test. Ask yourself, five times, "Why do I do this job?" and for each answer, ask, "And why is *that* important to me?" By the fifth "Why" you'll be getting closer to the truth of your purpose for doing the good work you perform.

6. **Preserve Energy and Enthusiasm:** Energy is the groundwork for enthusiasm; the only thing more contagious than enthusiasm is the *lack* of it! Practice daily strategies for taking care of your physical and emotional energy.

7. **Promise to Persevere:** You may be in the right job for you, and with the right organization, too, but still get into a funk sometimes. When you do, cut yourself some slack and persevere. Blue periods usually disappear sooner or later. Keep the faith. Make a list of the things that you love about your work (and then keep that list close by to look at every now and then).

8. **Perpetuate Relationships:** Find creative, time efficient ways to stay in touch with your circle of influence, and expand the

circle regularly. Network. Keep in touch with enthusiastic, energized colleagues in your field, and even outside your field, to help sustain your passion for your profession. Be sure to attend and champion employer-supported internal conferences. Attend some external professional association conferences where possible, too! Professional conferences and formal developmental workshop opportunities can make a *big* difference in what happens next in your career or life!

What we call the beginning is often the end

And to make an end is to make a beginning.

The end is where we start from...

We shall not cease from exploration

And the end of all our exploring

Will be to arrive where we started

And know the place for the first time...

— T. S. Eliot, *Four Quartets (Little Gidding)*

And one last time, with an "I" instead of a "you"...

If I always do what I've always done, I'll always get what I've always got. — Anonymous

This is such a profound message and it's a good quote, too! If you *really* want something different and more positive out of the experience of your workdays, you've got to...*do something different!* When it comes to what you do for a living, right now in the present day, what can you do to "take this job and love it" a little more? to experience it differently? *Decide* to do something different, even if it's just one little thing. Make a commitment; a promise to yourself to put even *one* of these eight strategies to work. Revive your *joie de vivre!* After all, you spend a lot of time—a lot of your *life* at work—so live for the weekdays as well as the weekends!

It's your *life*, right now. It's happening *now*, so make it count. It's *not* a dress rehearsal! Whether you sit in the CEO's seat or perform a routine, entry-level function, make the most of your work by folding passion into your profession everyday. You owe it to yourself to enjoy and get pleasure—and, yes, even passion—from the good work you do, to feel alive, to feel the pleasure of your fine contribution to the whole...to make a difference.

Easier Said Than Done?

If you argue for your limitations, you get to keep them.
— Richard Bach

Yes, I know, I know, some will dismiss what I suggest, give excuses for keeping the status quo and not even *try* to rediscover passion for their work. But note that the saying isn't, "Easier said, *impossible* to do", it's just *easier* to say something than to do something.

It *can* be done. You *can* infuse your work—any work—with passion and positive focus. Be *proud* of your work, and passionate about it, too! It's nice to hear some praise from on high once in a while, but it's not *necessary* for getting passion out of your profession. You can stir that up all on your own. I'm reminded of a comic strip showing a robust, senior executive-type man sitting in a throne-like chair, behind a grand oak desk, addressing a meek, round shouldered employee standing before him. The caption reads, "I'd *like* to thank-you Harrison, but, as you well know, yours is a thankless job." Poor Harrison...no "thanks" is forthcoming for him from the "big cheese"..."the numero uno"! So what!

Indeed, it's certainly nice to receive kudos from others— bosses and clients/customers, alike—but if you don't (or if the frequency of "thanks" is too sparse for your liking), find your own ways to applaud yourself.

Here's one piece of inspiration and self-motivation that's worked for me for years:

The Paradoxical Commandments

People are illogical, unreasonable and self-centered.
Love them anyway.
If you do good, people will accuse you of selfish, ulterior motives.
Do good anyway.
If you are successful, you will win false friends and make true enemies.
Succeed anyway.
The good you do today will be forgotten tomorrow.
Do good anyway.
Honesty and frankness make you vulnerable.
Be honest and frank anyway.
The biggest men and women with the biggest ideas can be shot down by the smallest men and women with the smallest minds.
Think big anyway.
People favour underdogs but they follow only top dogs.
Fight for a few underdogs anyway.
What you spend days building may be destroyed overnight.
Build anyway.
People may really need your help but attack you if you help them.
Help people anyway.
Give the world the best you have and you get kicked in the teeth.
Give the world the best you have anyway.

— Kent M. Keith

Why embrace the "anyway" philosophy? Because *everything* in life counts! When you reach the end of your working days, how would you like to remember your investment of professional blood, sweat and tears? Would you regret that you hadn't given it all you had? Could you possibly find yourself saying, "If only I'd done more of this and less of that"? more peace keeping and smiling and less bellyaching? more harmonizing and less antagonizing? more "big picturing" and less nitpicking? Spare yourself that fate—that disapointment. Reconnect with your passion for whatever you do, *now*.

And so, dear reader, the time has come to close this chapter, this book and get on with whatever's in store for you *next*...at work and in life, because this much is true:

Life is change,

and *work* is change,

but *passion*—for your work and for your life—is *optional*, and each one of us gets to **choose**, so...

As you think about your decision to discover or rediscover *your* passion for your own fine profession, however humble or corner-office conspicuously grand, I leave you with the same call to action quote with which I opened this volume:

> *Make your choice adventurous stranger.*
> *Strike the bell and bide the danger.*
> *Or wonder 'til it drives you mad, what would have*
> *followed if you had.*
>
> — C. S. Lewis

What *would* have followed...if...you...had?

Class starts now!

Epilogue

A closing riddle for you: What do Michaelangelo, unmined diamonds, rubies and emeralds and the Latin word *educere* (from which *educate* is derived) have in common? I've heard it said that Michaelangelo never took full credit for his sculpted masterpieces. He believed that the beauty of any piece was always there—dormant and locked in stone; that his job was merely to chip away at that which was *not* the sculpted subject, so that the subject, in all its splendor and presence, could be revealed. Diamonds, rubies and emeralds exist deep in the earth, whether or not they're ever discovered. To behold these brilliant pieces of nature, one must *mine* them—dig them up! And *educere* means to "draw out". As an educator, this, in turn, means to realize that the pupil already has all the potential and wisdom for understanding, within. It's merely the educator's job to set up the learning experience in such a way that the pupil is *drawn out*, becomes aware and learns. With this philosophy in mind, I've entitled this book, *Getting Passion Out of Your Profession* (rather than Putting Passion Back *In*), so that you could dig up and draw out that which has always been there for you. I believe—and you probably know this for yourself, too— that your passion for the good work you perform is in there somewhere; after all, you *were* enthused when you first got the job, right? Then, for many, the long haul set in. Day-to-day workplace stressors, and the emotional and political uncertainties of our times, easily plucked away at the first bloom of excitement and passion for that new position. Can you relate to this? Perhaps you've spent time wondering if you could *ever* get back to your "early days" love of your job. The intent of this book was to set up a learning experience which would help you get back to your original level of enthusiasm, by way of embracing eight passion points, practiced daily. It's my hope that *Getting Passion Out of Your Profession* has helped you fan the embers of your workplace passion, and that you're now refueled and ready to go, go, go, with renewed enthusiasm for work and life, come what may.

Take advantage of substantial discounts when you purchase multiple copies of *Getting Passion Out of Your Profession.*

A valuable resource for everyone in your group, organization, company or professional association. Although primarily applicable to people focusing on getting passion out of their *professions,* this book is applicable to one's private life, too!

For both professional *and* personal development and growth, *Getting Passion Out of Your Profession* serves as an inspiring, easy-to-apply reference. *"Getting Passion..."* is suitable for distribution in quantity by executives, managers, training professionals, organizational development consultants and association event planners, to help people throughout their organizations learn how to:

- choose positive language to shift attitude and behaviour in self and others

- acknowledge and declare professional self-worth

- foster a sense of humour for spirit and passion, as well as health and wellness

- identify and sever the anger cycle in self and others

- modify personal perspective to deal with changeable workplace "weather"

- gain clarity about bigger picture professional purpose

- maintain physical and emotional energy

- persevere during trying times

- and nurture and grow professional relationships

Getting Passion Out of Your Profession **also makes a terrific gift for** young adults just starting out in their first job opportunities or careers; individuals dabbling with the idea of changing careers or shifting choices; people coping with major changes or crisis; those who have been down-sized or have seen their job descriptions altered dramatically; people feeling plateaued, bored or in a funk; managers, entrepreneurs and executives aiming to further develop their mastery at interpersonal communications and leadership inspiration; anyone, anywhere open to further evolving their attitudes, behaviours, demonstrations and beliefs for greater day-to-day satisfaction, wherever they go; customers, clients, colleagues, suppliers, distributors and other workplace or business partners with whom you daily interact.

Major discounts are available for multiple copies of *Getting Passion Out of Your Profession*. Visit Nina Spencer & Associates' website www.ninaspencer.com or call 416-588-3334 for more information.

Keynotes & Workshops with Nina Spencer

Nina Spencer is one of Canada's most dynamic, authentic and thought-provoking female professional business and motivational speakers. Her powerful wisdom and spot-on insights on workplace leadership, interpersonal communications, adjusting to change, work-life balance, professional self-worth, employee and self-motivation, service excellence, team building, dealing with difficult people, conflict and stress management, presentation skills and, most of all, (re)building workplace passion, have made her the first choice of organizations and associations in Canada and abroad, seeking a quality and truly *professional* conference keynote speaker or workshop facilitator. Nina Spencer's magical mix of solid content, humour and entertainment helps transform professional lives and restore workplace commitment in these seemingly ever-turbulent times. Nina Spencer thoroughly researches and customizes each keynote or workshop presentation so that each client and each participant experiences a maximum opportunity to reach new levels of personal performance, passion, creativity, communication mastery and workplace fulfillment. She is consistently ranked highly at a wide diversity of annual professional association conferences and in-house company or organization staff events, in both the private and public sectors.

Working effectively and enthusiastically with frontline and management staff alike—as well as entrepreneurs—Nina Spencer's clients include:

Xerox, Whirlpool, McDonalds, Bombardier, Rogers, Sprint, Telus, ScotiaMcLeod, RBC, BMO, Ellis Don, Levi Strauss, Royal LePage, Maple Leaf Foods, Korn Ferry International, Enbridge Gas, Torys LLP, Novartis, Glaxo, AMGEN, FTD International, Old Port Cigar Compagny, Rothmans Benson & Hedges, Mercer Management, Trillium Health Centre, University Health Network, City of Mississauga, as well as numerous government ministries, regional municipalities, agencies, school boards and other educational institutions.

Nina's association clients include: Canadian Society of Association Executives, Meeting Professionals International, Canadian Association of Women Executives and Entrepreneurs, Human Resources Professionals Association of Ontario, Canadian Professional Sales Association, Promotional Products Association of Canada, International

Association Administrative Professionals, Conference Board of Canada, Certified General Accountants of Ontario, Ontario Hospital Association, Canadian Diabetes Association, Arthritis Society of Canada, Alberta Association of Optometrists, Association of Municipal Managers, Clerks and Treasurers of Ontario, Municipal Finance Officers' Association of Ontario, Union of Nova Scotia Municipalities, Institute of Law Clerks of Ontario, Ontario Long Term Care Association and Parks and Recreation Ontario. Since 1998, Nina has also repeatedly facilitated workshops for: staff and faculty of the University of Guelph, and public management development workshops in partnership with the Canadian Management Centre and the American Management Association.

A recurring guest of radio and television programs such as CTV's *Report on Business Television,* CITY's *Breakfast Television* and CBC 1, Nina Spencer has also profiled by publications such The Globe and Mail, National Post, Financial Post, Toronto Star, Oakland Tribune, Ottawa Citizen, Edmonton Journal, Calgary Herald, Hamilton Spectator, Reader's Digest, and Profit, Macleans, Canadian Business and Chatelaine Magazines, as well as numerous professional trade publications.

If you are searching for excellence in a keynote speaker or professional development workshop facilitator for senior management, independent contributors or frontline staff—a knowledgeable, warm and genuine presenter who is very easy to work with behind the scenes and knows *how* to reach a diversity of audiences—Nina Spencer is a rare find, indeed! With her energetic, informative and unique perspectives, Nina will help make your next meeting, conference or professional development workshop a long-to-be-remembered experience.

**To book Nina Spencer for your next conference
or in-house event please visit:**

www.ninaspencer.com or,
alternatively, email: **nina@ninaspencer.com**; or
please also feel free to call: **416-588-3334**

Keep Your Passion Alive, Come What May by Subscribing to the Complimentary On-line *Working Wisdom* Newsletter at... www.ninaspencer.com

Visit **www.ninaspencer.com** for years of back-issues of Nina's highly regarded and widely read complimentary, on-line publication, *Working Wisdom.*

Working Wisdom offers tried and tested strategies, quick tips and easy-to-facilitate ideas and exercises for improved professional passion, workplace communications and productivity.

www.ninaspencer.com also offers comprehensive information about Nina's:

- diversity of clients

- other articles published

- applause and accolades

- calendar of events/keynote and workshop engagements

- most popular keynote topics

- "Nina in the News"

- a selection of audio and video clips of presentations, and...

- detailed down-loadable biography, as well as...

- other information about Nina Spencer & Associates and services offered

Share Your Passion Prose

Nina Spencer would love to hear how this book has affected both you and your organization. Share your insights, success stories, experiences and tales of (re)newly discovered professional passion that have surfaced because of reading and applying one or *all* of the passion points offered in *Getting Passion Out of Your Profession.* Contact Nina by email **nina@ninaspencer.com** or via **www.ninaspencer.com**. Nina will make every effort to respond to you with a personal note.

Index

V

W

Y

Z

About the Author

Profiled by The National Post as, "One of Canada's leading motivational speakers" (in an article reviewing, *Getting Passion Out of Your Profession*, at the time of its realease in February, 2006), Nina Spencer is a seasoned, but not too marinated, keynote speaker, workshop facilitator, retreat leader, teacher, writer and author. One of Canada's most sought-after professional business and inspirational presenters, she's been "at it" since 1979 and so shares almost three decades of corporate and organizational development wisdom, insights and expertise every time out. Nina lives in downtown Toronto, in a century old home, with her family, sweet Soft-Coated Wheaten Terrier "puppy" Angus and other wondrous, assorted family pets.